Merle Alliso

SERMONS FOR

CHRISTIAN SEASONS

Abingdon
Nashville

Sermons for Christian Seasons

Copyright © 1976 by Abingdon

Library of Congress Cataloging in Publication Data

Johnson, Merle Allison
    Sermons for Christian seasons.

    1. Church year sermons.   2. Methodist Church—
Sermons.   3. Sermons, American.   I. Title.
BX8333.J58S47   252'.6   75-44210

ISBN 0-687-37809-5

MANUFACTURED BY THE PARTHENON PRESS AT
NASHVILLE, TENNESSEE, UNITED STATES OF AMERICA

For Marsha,
Karla,
Lisa,
Cindy,
Julie,
and
Lance—
Rachel's children
who are especially dear to me.

Preface

This effort marks my second attempt at a book of sermons. The first book, *Ancient Fires for Modern Man,* made me feel indebted to persons too numerous to mention. They were those wonderful people who had stimulated my mind as I went through the Old Testament stories. The situation remains the same at the present. No man can be certain that he has anything new at all to say.

These sixteen sermons represent to the best of my knowledge my own ideas. Yet, I can never be sure that some church school teacher, some former pastor, or someone I once heard or read did not say these things first. Though I have made every effort possible to document borrowed material, it is impossible to trace the germination of every thought.

Therefore, I am a man in debt and I shall try to repay some of this debt. I hope that fellow ministers who labor as I have with the written word may profit from these ideas. So many, many preachers have helped me and in this small way I would like to help others. While some of the sermons technically may not fit the exact Christian season, they are intended for general seasonal emphasis. In my own pulpit work I try to stay with the emphasis of the particular time of the Christian Year, but I am not slavish in following the exact texts. These sermons have come from the seasons of joy, and I hope they can be so used.

Again, I express gratitude to my helpful secretaries, Helen Bayles and Mary Walker, and especially to Virginia Buck, who assisted in the detail of the final revision.

Contents

For Advent—*The Hope of His Coming*

For Lent—*The Shadow of His Cross*

For Eastertide—*The Light of His Resurrection*

For Pentecost—*The Leadership of His Spirit*

FOR ADVENT

The Hope of His Coming

The Man Who Only Wanted Word

"Now when Jesus was born in Bethlehem of Judea in the days of Herod the king, behold, wise men from the East came to Jerusalem, saying, 'Where is he who has been born king of the Jews? For we have seen his star in the East, and have come to worship him.' When Herod the king heard this, he was troubled, and all Jerusalem with him; and assembling all the chief priests and scribes of the people, he inquired of them where the Christ was to be born. They told him, 'In Bethlehem of Judea; for so it is written by the prophet: "And you, O Bethlehem, in the land of Judah, are by no means least among the rulers of Judah; for from you shall come a ruler who will govern my people Israel." ' Then Herod summoned the wise men secretly and ascertained from them what time the star appeared; and he sent them to Bethlehem, saying, 'Go and search diligently for the child, and when you have found him bring me word, that I too may come and worship him' " (Matt. 2:1-8).

This is the first Sunday in the season of the Christian Year that we begin to center our thoughts on the birth of Jesus. In a broader scope this season beckons us to think of the second as well as the first coming of our Lord. Never have there been words so stained with cunning and drenched in malice as those of Herod when he said to the wise men, "Go and make every effort to find out about the little child and when you have found Him, send news to me, that I, too, may come and worship Him."

Before we talk about some very fundamental elements of the confrontation of Herod with the news of Jesus' birth, let us think about this man Herod. Herod was half-Jew and half-Idumean. This had historical overtones which made for a terrible combination of heritage. It was terrible both because the two sides of his parentage were bitter enemies, and because the malignant union was to set the course of his life—a nightmare of treachery that has characterized few other men. Herod was first appointed governor by the Romans and then became the Jewish king.

He was called Herod the Great, and to his credit he did keep peace in his country. This was accomplished, however, by exacting capital punishment for the smallest of petty crimes, making most folks fearful for their lives. He could be a generous man at times. One such occasion found him melting down some of his gold in order to buy food for some starving people.

His chief fault was his paranoid nature. This drove him to insane acts. He was called a "murderous old man" by one contemporary historian. Anyone he became suspicious of was summarily eliminated. He executed his wife and her mother and three of his sons. This prompted the Roman Emperor Augustus to make his famous statement, "It is safer to be Herod's pig than Herod's son."

Probably the most notorious of his policies involved certain provisions he made just before his death at age seventy. At this time, he moved to Jericho, the loveliest of all his cities. Remembering how Jerusalem hated him, he sent out orders that a list of the most prominent citizens of Jerusalem should be arrested on false charges. He ordered that the moment he died, they should all be put to death. He remarked that he was well aware that no one would mourn for his death and that he was determined that some tears should fall when he died.

Now, this is a brief sketch of the man who asked to be told where the young child lay under the pretense that he wanted to come and worship him. Sherman Johnson in his exegesis of Matthew in volume 7, page 256 of *The Interpreter's Bible* (Nashville: Abingdon Press, 1951) suggests that this scene presents the enigma of history: "How does goodness survive when badness has both conspiracy and the sword?" In answer, Johnson paraphrases then quotes an excerpt from "The Present Crisis" by James Russell Lowell. "Right may be on the scaffold and wrong on the throne, but 'standeth God within the shadow, keeping watch above his own.'"

In this image is represented the continuing drama of the forces of evil versus the forces of good. There are some lessons which ring true to our lives also. The first is:

Each man's worship must be preceded by his own search or it is not worth very much. Herod made the statement, "Go and search, and when you find him, then I'll come." This will not get the job done. The pilgrimage to a meaningful faith always involves a personal quest. All too often some men arrive at the time of commitment as a result of inferior motives or as a result of another man's search. This is, sad to say, representative of the state of the church all too often. There can be no reason for the disenchantment of people other than this one. Other things may surface and be blamed, but they are only superficial. The real reason for a living faith arises from a burning need that only this faith can satisfy. When men fall away from faith it is because they did not arrive as a result of a pilgrim's search or because their faith was not very genuine.

I must maintain that when men turn away from the church it is because they have a poor understanding of their need; and, since man's need for God cannot be extinguished, the only reason men do not have a meaningful faith is that *they are not on a meaningful search*. For example, literally thousands of young people have come into the church through routine classes of confirmation without having felt any genuine need. Also, the number of people who make superficial decisions during church demonstrations of revival techniques is staggering. On top of this, think of the many men who have joined as a result of a wife's pressure or perhaps a husband's insistence. One clergyman I know was in a baptistry preparing to immerse a man. As he began giving the last-minute instructions in a subdued voice to the candidate, he was startled when the man said to him, "Preacher, you better make this good because my wife has had you and every revival preacher call on me for years. Once I get out of here, maybe I'll have some peace but don't look for me to come back."

I think that we might say that this was something greatly less than commitment. Also, there are the many instances in which people have joined the church because of business pressure or social standing. When men sense their need for God they make peace with this need, and they will not deny it. When men deny faith it is because they never had faith. They never had saving faith because they never had the absolute experience of their *need of faith*. This is something deeper than belonging to a church. When men have made peace with these things, they will not be belligerent with the church, and the church's occasional hypocrisy will not destroy their faith.

Herod could never have worshiped Jesus as a result of another man's search, and neither can we. No one can bring you word about Jesus, you have to go see for yourself.

The second lesson to be derived from Herod's example is:

Vital Christian faith must have the element of experience. The ancient world knew this as well as Herod. The Eastern cultures were accustomed to shrines and places of worship. After a rational and meaningful search is underway there must arise the element of experience. Jesus told Nicodemus that he had to be born again. He had to experience a change. The God/man encounter involves experience, and this kind of experience is not only valid but necessary for a living faith. One does not have to dramatize it or demonstrate it in grotesque displays. Yet, in that secret chamber of the human heart Jesus meets a person, and his presence is unmistakable. What then is Christian experience?

In a saving experience man yields himself, and once this transaction is made, there is genuine conversion. Frances R. Havergal has written of man's proper attitude in the immortal words:

> Take my life, and let it be
> Consecrated, Lord, to thee. . . .
> Take my will, and make it thine;
> It shall be no longer mine.
> Take my heart, it is thine own;
> It shall be thy royal throne.
> Take my love; my Lord, I pour
> At thy feet its treasure store.
> Take myself, and I will be
> Ever, only, all for thee.   Amen.

Finally, Herod's insincerity meant that Christ would remain lost to him forever. Such was the case. The prophet speaking for God said "When you seek me with all your heart you shall find me." There was only one reason Herod never worshiped at Jesus' feet; he didn't want to. His search for Jesus was not due to need but to other reasons.

Christ remains hidden to those whose search stems from such motives as curiosity or vindictiveness. No man who ever wanted with all his heart to settle the question of faith was ever denied. The issue of Herod and all men is thus before us.

We have said today that the principle reason men repudiate their faith is that they never had one that was the result of a genuine search and a sincere and contrite heart. One day, years ago, I drove by a church Nativity scene with a likeness of the infant Jesus that seemed very real. I was shaken to discover upon close investigation that it was only a painted rock. I thought it would have been better had I remained at a distance. How horrible our gods appear when we look at them closely.

Paul said it for us "Even though we once regarded Christ from a human point of view, we regard him thus no longer. Therefore, if any one is in Christ, he is a new creation; the old has passed away, behold, the new has come" (II Cor. 5:16-17). A painted rock is a poor substitute for the living Lord. Men may repudiate their painted rocks, but they do not turn their backs on genuine commitment that easily. Even if they have grown cold and indifferent to their faith, if it is real faith they encountered, they will come back. If it was not real faith, we can only pray that they will turn and this time be genuinely converted.

"Bring me word . . ."—that will not do! The only way to find authentic faith is to seek it for ourselves.

12/9/90

The Man Who Said No, Then Yes

"In those days a decree went out from Caesar Augustus that all the world should be enrolled. This was the first enrollment, when Quirin'i-us was governor of Syria. And all went to be enrolled, each to his own city. And Joseph also went up from Galilee, from the city of Nazareth, to Judea, to the city of David, which is called Bethlehem, because he was of the house and lineage of David, to be enrolled with Mary, his betrothed, who was with child. And while they were there, the time came for her to be delivered. And she gave birth to her firstborn son and wrapped him in swaddling cloths, and laid him in a manger, because there was no place for them in the inn" (Luke 2:1-7).

Whenever great dramatic events are relived by the movement of time and man's yen for reenacting them, there always appears in the cast the villain and the hero. In fact, the recalling of any ancient drama seems to lose something unless we can identify the forces of evil and the personifications of good. This makes for good drama and realism in story telling.

This is the season of all seasons for that segment of the human family called Christian. The drama of that first Yuletide season is replayed each year with the accompaniment of visions of a day long ago when the restlessness of little Bethlehem was colored by beams of bright hope brought by the Christ child. The village was tense with angry people who were forced to sign the tax rolls. Although we talk of the impact of Christmas, to be quite frank, the birth of this baby didn't at first change the world very much. There were only a few people who were aware of the inner drama, and they were not clear about the exact meaning of this birth. We can think of its impact because we look back on it. For most of Bethlehem, his birth was inconsequential. *unimportant*

However, for us, this is the season of subdued voices and relaxed nerves—when men make extra efforts to be congenial. There is magic in this season—even Ebenezer Scrooge was changed. These are the days of lilting melodies —when songs are called by that lovely word carols. These are the times when men act better than they think they have the capacity to act. These are the days of every person's childhood when the world slowly begins its countdown to December the twenty-fifth.

The yearly recollection of this drama always brings to our minds the heroes and villains because a drama would not be complete without them. There is a villain other than Herod in this pageant—the man who said no and then said yes. He is the innkeeper. At the outset of this story let us approach this man exactly as the gospel writers approached him. We should see that they were not critical of him at all, in fact he was incidental to the story.

I too want to treat him with kindness, but not by absolving him from close scrutiny; for viewed objectively, *the innkeeper becomes a symbol of the frailty of all humankind, a representative of all those who compromise with doing the right thing.*

We should remember that he said there is no room in the inn and then said, "Yes, there is room in the stable." If he were a ~~prototype of~~ modern day innkeepers, we would all know that the "No vacancy" excuse was a cover.

Modern innkeepers always have a handful of rooms for dire emergency or for special customers. This is the rule of the trade, and while this may not be true in all cases, it surely is true in most. The little village was overcrowded with the steady stream of unhappy people coming to fill out the tax books. Mary's condition made Joseph go slower than the rest of the folks, and because of this, they arrived late.

To the innkeeper's credit, he said yes after saying no, but, he fell short of heeding the perfect standard, the golden rule. In those days women were treated with care just barely superior to animals. If the innkeeper were to have done the absolute best he could, he could have acted in one or two ways other than the the way he did act.

First of all, he could have given notice of Mary's condition to the many male room occupants and, if need be, commandeered a room for her. Surely there would have been one man in the large house who would have been willing to give a woman in this condition his room.

The second thing the innkeeper could have done was to give her his room. This would have been going the second mile.

Instead, like so many of his kinsmen through the centuries, he did just enough to salve his conscience and thus fell short of absolute selfless action. Any number of us will do the right thing up to a certain point, but no further. Or, we will do what is right if we are forced to; or, we will do what is right only as long as it doesn't cost us anything or involve us personally. Let us not overwork this comparison but, at the same time, let us not overlook the poignant truth that we are in the innkeeper's shoes all too often.

The innkeeper is also representative of those who base decisions about human interaction on regard for class

Do what pleases our peers

rather than for human need. Let us not be deluded, for the world has not changed in this respect. Joseph and Mary were peasants, and this was a very, very inexpensive hotel. If a man of rank had taken a pregnant woman to a high class establishment commensurate with his social standing we all know that the entire hierarchy would have rearranged itself to meet his need. If a man of wealth had come to this same innkeeper's hotel and, with all the trappings of wealth, had explained his plight, we know that the poor innkeeper would have been doubly flattered and would have made every effort to accommodate this family of rank. The truth of the matter is that he would have taken great pride in the fact that a prince was likely to be born on his premises.

Not so with the peasant carpenter Joseph and his suffering wife Mary. There were no signs either of wealth or rank or that their child would make any difference at all to the order of humanity—no, he would be just another baby in an already overpopulated country. The innkeeper was not a bad man, yet he was not truly good the way God intends that man be good. He was more than likely a slave to his world order. In vivid contrast to the man's actions toward Jesus' mother, Jesus throughout his lifetime had absolutely no regard for class—he responded first to human need. He gave the same attention to the woman of the streets that he did to the great man Nicodemus. In fact, the one aspect of Jesus' life that caused more discussion than any other one thing was his utter disregard for class.

Sadly enough the benefit of evenhandedness was not extended to the Jewish maiden, Mary. Again we should realize the bitter truth that we are in the innkeeper's shoes all too often.

In the third place, the innkeeper represents those who unknowingly refuse Jesus because they are preoccupied with the things of this life. I said "unknowingly" because it is not fair or honest to accuse this fellow of refusing to allow the Son of God to be born in his house. This is just the point. Had he known the circumstances, he would have acted accordingly. In one of the parables of Jesus a rich man died and went to Hell, and from Hell he cried out that if someone would tell his brothers of life's true design, they would not make his mistake.

I suppose this is true, but it is not the way life works. If God were to audibly call us by name and tell us his will at every crossroad, life would be easily conquered. But, then life would offer no real option; we would be overly influenced by the divine. Somehow in the mystery of it all we are left to live by the thin thread of faith and inner commitment to our Lord. We have eyes to see with, and we have ears to hear with. If through it all we are enamored and preoccupied with vain things, we become blinded by these things; and if we respond easily to the siren song of temptation, losing all ability to withstand it, we then become deafened to God's voice.

The truth of this story is that Jesus is always looking for a home. He is looking to be born or to become alive in each event of our lives. Happy is the marriage where Jesus is born into that union. Happy is the vocation where Jesus is born into the calling. Happy is the youth where Jesus is born into his or her choices. This story says, "Don't be so preoccupied with your own ways that Jesus can't be born into the situation."

The innkeeper said no, then yes, but it was not a good yes. I must tell you of the change Jesus made in one man at Christmas time. Some fifteen years ago I was in a country church at a revival meeting. We took a meal in a small house with a young man, his wife, and his three little children. On the way to the home, the minister told me that the house would be bare except for the basic essentials. The heartrending story was that on the eve of the previous Christmas, the couple and their three pre-school children had gone into town early to take the children's presents and other assorted gifts off layaway. The children had been so excited that they went in their sleeping garments.

With great joy the family returned home, only to face the horror of a scene of ashes—their home had burned and disintegrated due to a gas leak. Ironically, the young father had become a Christian only three weeks before that day.

I asked the pastor about the man's attitude, was he bitter? I was told that he carefully and tenderly gathered his stricken family about him and set about reestablishing his life with his small laborer's wages and inadequate insurance. When we walked through the bare front room to the kitchen where we ate, the young wife began to tell us the story. The hardest thing for her to bear was the loss of the year-old refrigerator on which the last payment had been made in November. During this story I was silently wondering, "Oh God, why did this happen to this young Christian family?" As I was musing, the young father answered me. He said, "Mr. Johnson, before I became a Christian we didn't have a home. We had a house. After I became a Christian we had a home even though we lost a house. You may not believe it, but it was the happiest Christmas of our lives." I could have wept with the emotion of the moment, and I couldn't say a word. Remember this carol?

> Oh, come to my heart, Lord Jesus,
> There is room in my heart for thee.

A Song to Lowly Men

"And in that region there were shepherds out in the field, keeping watch over their flock by night. And an angel of the Lord appeared to them, and the glory of the Lord shone around them, and they were filled with fear. And the angel said to them, 'Be not afraid, for behold, I bring you good news of a great joy which will come to all the people; for to you is born this day in the city of David a Savior, who is Christ the Lord. And this will be a sign for you: you will find the babe wrapped in swaddling cloths and lying in a manger.' And suddenly there was with the angel a multitude of the heavenly host praising God and saying, 'Glory to God in the highest, and on earth peace among men with whom he is pleased!' When the angels went away from them into heaven, the shepherds said to one another, 'Let us go over to Bethlehem and see this thing that has happened, which the Lord has made known to us.' And they went with haste, and found Mary and Joseph, and the babe lying in a manger. And when they saw it they made known the saying which had been told them concerning the child; and all who heard it wondered at what the shepherds told them. But Mary kept all these things, pondering them in her heart. And the shepherds returned, glorifying and praising God for all they had heard and seen, as it had been told them. And at the end of eight days, when he was circumcised, he was called Jesus, the name given by the angel before he was conceived in the womb" (Luke 2:8-21).

Time, beyond all else in this life, is the most astounding of mysteries. In fact, there is in one sense an impossibility of defining what time is. It is only roughly defined as the period between two given points.

To children time crawls, but to adults time goes by so swiftly it is almost cruel. The enchantment of Christmas Day is almost here and will be gone all too quickly. Its magic holds us in its power for a moment, but then the harsh world of competitiveness sets in again.

The classic phrase for this season in the New Testament is, "In the fullness of time, God sent his son." This was the understanding of the early church—that the time was just right for Christ to be born. The characters who played prominent parts in this drama are easy to remember. Most every child has been in a Christmas pageant and has had to wear an old bath robe in pretense of being a shepherd or a wise man. Little girls have carried angel wings ceremoniously on their backs. In the Christmas story the characters all fit; it seems as if there would have been no other options. Essential to the story of Jesus' birth are the roles of angels and shepherds and wise men. We can't imagine the story without these characters.

Today, let us think about those few shepherds who speak so loudly to all the world at this time. In a world in which electronic devices make the noises which grab our attention, the shepherds still have something to say to us. There is a commonness to these men and a commonality which makes it easy for us to identify with them.

We ought to clear the air somewhat at this stage and say a word about the image of the shepherds. Shepherding and the pastoral life in the days of David was a very noble calling. The Twenty-Third Psalm was written against the backdrop of a life to be greatly admired. But things had changed in the thousand years before the angels spoke to these certain shepherds. Travel and commerce were opening up as never before in the first century world. As a result, bands of road gangs and thieves would rob and plunder at will, and there were few, if any, patrols to police the country.

Whether it was a proven fact or not, the shepherds were accused of most of this highway banditry. And so, the life of a shepherd by the time of Jesus' birth was considered a suspect vocation. We don't know much in the way of detail about the shepherds of our story, but what the total picture says to us speaks loudly and is unmistakably clear. *The most obvious thing of all is that the heavenly announcement was made to religious nonprofessionals.*

It is a fact that God speaks to men through events and signs. This is the way he has chosen to communicate throughout the years. It is also true that the gospel writers chose to speak through stories of men. These facts being irrefutably true, just what are the gospel storytellers trying to say to us. What does the angelic announcement mean?

One answer is on the surface. The priests had become oblivious to the old prophecies. Consequently, they might have dismissed the appearance of the angels as a bizarre dream. Unbelieving persons are seldom sensitive to heavenly voices, whether they speak out loud or through events. This is most often the case with us. When Herod asked the priests about the prophecy, they said they knew that the Messiah was to be born in Bethlehem. So they knew— or at least some did—but the sad fact is that those who knew were not interested in pursuing the old prophecy.

We may conclude, then, that though some persons have access to the knowledge of the spiritual, they will not pursue it at all. Here is an interesting point. Persons scarcely ever start from zero; they usually have something in the way of fact or experience to go on in their search for the truth of God. Thus, the problem with many people is not that they are starting with a scientifically sterile and uncluttered viewpoint (they have been through many experiences a long way down the road), but that they, under pretense of doubt, will not act on the evidence they have. Such was the plight of the religious establishment when Jesus was born. Its members had the prophecies before them; they simply chose to ignore them!

There is yet another reason the priests were not the recipients of angelic announcements. They were in that most terrible of predicaments; they had a religious front but a Godless religion. There is such a thing, and it is frightening. I read this past week of a resurgence of interest in the spiritual life of inward devotion and prayer on the part of a segment of the church universal. The writer spoke with great joy at the prospects that once again his wing of the church was interested in the inner relationship of God and man. The question that kept running through my mind was "What on earth *have* you been doing?" But, I knew the answer.

Every so often the religious establishment gets caught up in good humanitarian causes and often, unfortunately, at the expense of its central purpose. If the church fails here, the church has failed. It doesn't make any difference how powerful it is as a political lobbyist or a force for good, it will not last. The church either has a message to man about God or it doesn't really have anything unique to say at all. The burden of religion has always been to clarify in man's mind his relationship to God, and then it can speak clearly about man's relationship to man.

The shepherds heard the heavenly announcement and the religious establishment didn't because the religious pros wouldn't know what the angels were talking about. Such a strange twist of events. Remember the spiritual "Sweet little Jesus boy, they didn't know who you was." Such was the case in century one—could it happen today?

There is another interpretation of this event—*its im-*

plication of life's simplicity. We talk of life as being complex and it is—oh, how it is. Yet, this story says that simple, common men received the most complex of truths, the announcement of the birth of the Savior. The story of Jesus is a drama from beginning to end. It is one huge event which speaks a word—a single word to all mankind. Notice, the angel said, "Unto you is born this day a Savior which is Christ the Lord." The word *Christ* means "Messiah," a word which signified the person God chose for a specific task. The work he was to do was the work of saving men, of making them new.

Now, the field of theology is admittedly the most complex field in literary halls. The biblical documents must be studied in the most exacting way to ascertain the meaning of the early languages. But, having said that, let me follow the implication of simplicity which surfaces here. These shepherds could understand the angel's message, and if they could, maybe the writer is saying first that the event of Christ is simply understood when one opens his mind and heart to it and secondly that this is possible for all men.

The truth of this life is that man needs Christ the Savior. Man needs to be saved from this world. That is not too hard to understand. By world, I mean the total sum of influences and experiences that confront men on their journey. The simple fact is that the world will overcome a man—a man can't cope with it through his own strength. The wisest have become the chiefest cynics; the noblest have become the fallen; and the great ones have been brought to horrible depths. We need to be saved from this world.

Man needs to be saved from himself. That is not an unlearned assessment. To the contrary, it is a valid truth that, left to ourselves, you and I would do ourselves in. The New Testament calls these ideas by various versions of the word "sin." For whatever it is worth to those who do not like to simplify life, Jesus came to do something for us we couldn't do for ourselves. It is the simple truth that he, and he only, can save his people from their sins.

There is a third point: *There is the beautiful picture of the hurried response of guileless men.* One of them said, "Come let us go and see this thing which has come to pass." "Let us go." "Let us go." These were men without guile. Guile is that characteristic which allows us to posture in one way and think another way. It is hypocrisy, which is to act one way in one place and act the opposite in other environs. By their guileless attitude these men indicated their capacity for true religion. The positive response to all true religion is, "Come, let us go and do what is right." In our private life where each of us has his own unique relationship with God, only we know how honest is that life.

The entire business—from the invocation to the benediction, the steeple to the basement—is to enhance and make more real this God/man relationship. We try to bring it to birth in conversion and confession; we try to cultivate it through worship, Christian education, prayer, inspiration and programming. But the truth of the matter is that all of us sit on a lonely hillside dozing over the business of life, and when the truths of God are spoken in unmistakably angelic clarity, only we and God really know our true response. Many men come away from their hillsides wearing a facade of great perplexity, but I wonder, I wonder—was God not clear?

It is not that God has not spoken to us in simplicity, it is that we are not always willing to say, "Come, let us go and do what is right." There is huge complexity to this life, but there is no confusion when we seek to go home to God. The way home has been clearly shown to us in Christ.

About this same time before Christmas several years ago now, I remember late one grey winter day when a knock came on my office door. I was to spend fully one hour in the presence of a transient, a hobo of the highways. After the customary stories he noticed something that prompted him to shed his facade—a book, I believe.

In that hour, I was to hear a story as lucid as one could hear from a well-educated man. He gave a resumé of Christian theology with an understanding few laymen have. He had been a college professor; I gained from what he said that life just did him in. No great tragedy, just life! He confessed that he had never joined a church or professed a faith, but, that he was conversant on the matter, I could plainly see. He knew about faith, but he had not experienced faith. He knew about Jesus, but only from a distance. I asked him if he would like to accept the way home by becoming a Christian. He said no. As I watched him go I could hear the words, "I am the light of the world, he who follows me shall not walk in darkness but shall have the light of life." The reason the angels didn't speak to the priests is they were like that man.

J. S. Whale, the eminent Anglican theologian said "Instead of putting off our shoes from our feet because the place where we stand is holy ground, we are taking nice photographs of the burning bush from suitable angles; we are chatting about theories of Atonement with our feet on the mantlepiece, instead of kneeling down before the wounds of Christ" (*Christian Doctrine* [Cambridge: At the University Press, 1941] p. 152).

In contrast to this we cannot help but notice that the lowly shepherds came and fell down at the place where the Christ child lay. That is true religion, "Come, let us go quickly and see this thing which has come to pass." Has anything come to pass recently in your heart?

Come, let us go quickly!

Rachel's Children

"Then Herod, when he saw that he had been tricked by the wise men, was in a furious rage, and he sent and killed all the male children in Bethlehem and in all that region who were two years old or under, according to the time which he had ascertained from the wise men. Then was fulfilled what was spoken by that prophet Jeremiah: 'A voice was heard in Ramah, wailing and loud lamentation, Rachel, weeping for her children; she refused to be consoled, because they were no more'" (Matt. 2:16-18).

When we think of Christmas, we think of children. Red, yellow, black, and white, they are all precious in our sight— the children of the world at Christmas. Christmas belongs to the children; it is heaven-made for them. I hardly know how to get into the sermon today because it could be difficult to make you feel what I feel. I want to preach about the relationship of children to the Biblical story of the first Christmas. I have chosen to call this sermon "Rachel's Children."

When Matthew set about writing the story of Jesus' birth, he found three significant events in the infancy of Jesus that he saw as fulfilled predictions from the Old Testament.

The first was the parallel he saw between the nation Israel in Egyptian captivity and Joseph taking Mary and the baby into Egypt to escape the wrath of Herod. Herod had ordered the execution of all the male children under two years of age. He hoped in this way to do away with Jesus. He had been told that a mysterious child had been born who was to be king. He searched in vain for the child, and when he did not find him, he ordered the massacre.

When Joseph heard that Herod was dead, he came back home to Israel from Egypt. Matthew saw a parallel in Joseph's bringing the baby Jesus from Egypt to Moses' bringing the entire nation home. In between these events, the prophet Hosea, commenting about the Moses experience, called the nation Israel, God's son. Hosea says "God called his son out of Egypt." So Matthew, knowing both the Moses story and Hosea's symbolic description of it, sees in Jesus a stunning fulfillment of this sequence. "Out of Egypt have I called my son," he says.

Then he makes a similar allusion when Jesus is taken to Nazareth to live. We are not certain what ancient idea he had in mind, nevertheless, he saw in this fact a fulfillment of the idea that Jesus would be referred to as the Nazarene.

The third idea Matthew uses is the most graphic because it is filled with pathos. When Herod ordered the execution of the male children, the nation went into a hysteria of grief. Matthew thought of another Old Testament idea which paralleled this.

In the book of Jeremiah, the Israelites are depicted in the midst of their exile to Babylon. As they march in their long procession, they pass Ramah, which was the place where Rachel was buried. Rachel was Jacob's wife. Remember that Jacob was later called Israel. His twelve sons became the heads of the twelve tribes of Israel. Rachel is the mother figure of Israel.

As the Israelites pass Rachel's tomb, Jeremiah pictures a living Rachel sitting weeping over her children being taken to a prisoner of war camp. Matthew remembers Jeremiah's statement about Rachel's weeping, and when Herod begins the mass execution of the children, he makes the statement, "Rachel is weeping again for her children."

In a wondrous way all children are God's children, and that makes them Rachel's children. Rachel is still weeping over her children because the Herods are still alive.

There is one especially good reason we ought to love little children, and that is—they didn't ask to come here. I want you to notice three things about Rachel's children and the Herods of the world.

In the first place the little children were affected by one man's insecurity. They still are! Herod was so insecure as king that he allowed himself to really believe that an infant could challenge him.

I know of a lot of insecure Herods. They say: "Since the baby came you have not shown me as much attention." They say, "Since the baby came, we don't go out as often as we used to, and I miss it." They say: "I'm sick of being cooped up in this house with these kids all day long." They say, "If I had known the trouble that having a baby brings, I never would have wanted one."

I know a lot of female as well as male Herods. They have never grown up and affirmed their own adulthood, and the children threaten them because *they* want to remain children in a child's world where they need not be responsible. Rachel is weeping because of what man's insecurity does to her children.

In the second place the children were affected by mankind's inhumanity. They still are. I read a lot about the Herods who are yet with us. They are still inhuman to the little children. They hire them for wages far too small under the pretext of "They need the work." The Herods sit in the chairs of big business and make clothing for children that is fire hazardous—clothing that has caused children to be burned beyond recognition.

I read about the parental Herods in this country who by the thousands each day torture Rachel's children. They don't go to prison because of weak child abuse laws or other legal loopholes. After all, their children are theirs— what business do outsiders have with other people's children? So the children are left to be beaten and burned with cigarettes.

Little children are really not human to some people unless they are white. To the Herods, they are different somehow. They are nigger kids, Japs, Wops, Jews, and filthy Indians. Herod said, "Kill them all!" and the Herods keep saying that to this day.

I read about a Herod recently who in an American uniform turned a machine gun on a row of little girls and boys. I saw the horrified look on their faces right before they died. The camera man was there. That Herod was a hero to many. I buried a Green Beret lieutenant who volunteered to go back for another hitch of duty to work with the Montagnard people. I read his last letter telling of his belief that he was doing something useful. Soon after this letter a sniper cut him down. He was there working with the children less than a hundred miles away when the other man killed those Vietnamese children. He was a different kind of man than that other. Rachel's children are continually abused by mankind's inhumanity.

In the third place, the environment affects Rachel's children. Even the baby Jesus was moved to Nazareth so he could be in a better place to live. The Herods don't care for the children. They will corrupt their environment with filth in literature, movies, TV, and other media of communication if they can. They will make dope addicts of grade school children if we are silent. Let us not sell short the factor of a good environment.

The standards of a nation are best shown by what it allows to take place with Rachel's children. The greatest crime of all is a crime against a child. Society is too lenient with the Herods, and that is why Rachel continues to cry. As a whole, the nation could have overthrown Herod, but it did not. It stood by and let Herod slaughter the children.

Every time I see child abuse, broken homes, narcotics traffic, I ask myself what I can do. I realize that many of the Herods sit in church. I wonder what they have been hearing. I have mentioned only a few ways in which men abuse children; you can supply others. All of Christian history is filled with the efforts of the church to help Rachel dry her tears. Jesus is pictured in many loving ways, but the dearest of all postures was when he took a child and put it on his knee. That went a long way toward helping Rachel dry her eyes. Jesus' people have all loved the little children. They distinguish themselves in this way. Christmas makes it a better world for Rachel's children. The first Christmas touched the lives of little children more than we ever imagined. Jesus still does. Do you remember this song by Jemima T. Luke?

> I think when I read that sweet story of old,
> When Jesus was here among men,
> How He called little children as lambs to His fold,
> I should like to have been with them then.
> I wish that His hands had been placed on my head,
> That His arms had been thrown around me,
> And that I might have seen His kind look when He said,
> "Let the little ones come unto me."
> Yet still to His footstool in prayer I may go,
> And ask for a share in His love;
> And if I thus earnestly seek Him below,
> I shall see Him and know Him above.   Amen.

FOR LENT

The Shadow of His Cross

That First Palm Sunday

"And when they drew near to Jerusalem and came to Beth'phage, to the Mount of Olives, then Jesus sent two disciples, saying to them, 'Go into the village opposite you, and immediately you will find an ass tied, and a colt with her; untie them and bring them to me. If any one says anything to you, you shall say, "The Lord has need of them" and he will send them immediately.' This took place to fulfill what was spoken by the prophet, saying, 'Tell the daughter of Zion, Behold, your king is coming to you, humble, and mounted on an ass, and on a colt, the foal of an ass.' The disciples went and did as Jesus had directed them; they brought the ass and the colt, and put their garments on them, and he sat thereon. Most of the crowd spread their garments on the road, and others cut branches from the trees and spread them on the road. And the crowds that went before him and that followed him shouted, 'Hosanna to the Son of David! Blessed is he who comes in the name of the Lord! Hosanna in the highest!' And when he entered Jerusalem, all the city was stirred, saying, 'Who is this?' And the crowds said, 'This is the prophet Jesus from Nazareth of Galilee' " (Matt. 21:1-11).

On the Sunday before Jesus was crucified, he made a sudden appearance in Jerusalem. We must remember that for many days he had been in hiding at this stage of his ministry. He was considered an outlaw, and a reward had been offered for his capture. Yet he made his own choice to come out into the open, to permit himself to be captured, and to undergo the agony of a trial and death by crucifixion.

Jerusalem was a seething cauldron of emotions at this particular time. This was the Jewish Passover celebration and the loyal Israelites came from every corner of the land and even from outside the national boundaries. This was a time of intense nationalistic pride; a Jewish fourth of July. The Passover commemorated the Jewish exodus from slavery in Egypt.

Certainly we can ask why Jesus chose to go into the city at such a time as this, although the biographers do not provide us with reasons. Perhaps he wanted to confront the Jewish nation and claim his kingdom. There are other speculations, but the one I favor is that he knew that death would be imminent; therefore, he chose to die when the celebration would be centered around the figure of the paschal lamb. By comparing himself to the lamb he could literally fulfill the ancient ritual with his own death.

He is seen riding into town on the back of a donkey belonging to one of his followers. The crowds threw branches with palm leaves in his pathway. This was a ritual they performed on many occasions. The term "Hosanna" means "Save now!" Obviously, they were urging him to set up a national kingdom at that moment. Their flag-waving broke his heart, and he went out by himself and wept over the city. This story opens up several pertinent avenues of thought.

There is first of all the fickleness with which many approach Jesus. His followers were not the first people to try to make him into something he was not. They wanted to make him a king, and that he was, but not in the same way they dreamed of royalty. Their acclamations were tantamount to a landslide draft by a political party or to

34

the backing of a favorite son. Jesus would not yield to this form of pressure. Closely related to this attitude was their effort to make him into a crusader, an opponent of all the social and political ills of the country. They were tired of the oppressive heel of Rome, for they were a captive people, always under an uneasy martial law. Now they saw their chance for a leader. Again Jesus refused to acquiesce. This age seems to be one for crusaders also, and Jesus has again become the prime example of this sort of thing. There are many wrongs which need to be made right, but now, as then, Jesus is not a proper model for this role. He was no social crusader as such. His gospel revolutionized society, but it changed individual men's lives first.

Then there is the category of a religious example. Many saw in Jesus the supreme example of a good and pious Jew, a type of hero for young men to emulate. Such was the fickleness of the crowd—they placed him in the wrong categories.

There is another type of fickleness; and, paradoxically, this is the other extreme. There were those in the crowd, as there are those today, who have Jesus in the proper category; they are orthodox in their understanding of Jesus. There is no conflict here. However, there is also no commitment. This is the dilemma of the church all too often. Most of the unresponsive members in congregations believe the right things about Jesus but are fickle and lukewarm in their commitment.

This leads us to a real conclusion in this matter. Ultimately, it is not one's relationship to the church that is primary; it is one's relationship with Jesus. First things come first, and when a man is right with the Lord, he will be right with the church. The problem is never a problem of man and the church. It is a problem of a man and his Lord. When a man is right with his Lord, he will find a way to be right with his church; and if his church is wrong, the church can be made right, but only if the people committed to Jesus make it right. We make many mistakes as churches. I can't speak for every minister, but I can speak for most because of my experience. If there is a hindrance to your total commitment to your church, then your minister will want to hear of it and so will your church. You will never solve your disagreement with the institutional church by staying away from it.

I think of D. L. Moody's story of the man who was a committed Christian yet did not want to be part of a church. They were sitting in front of a fire, and Moody raked a live coal away from the flame. In a minute it went out. Moody pointed to the dead coal. The man said—"I see."

The second thing we notice about Jesus' entry into Jerusalem is that the eternal question arises. "Who is this man?" some of the crowd asked. They had surely heard of him, but they had not seen him in person. This is a question men can't escape. This is the great question in *Jesus Christ Superstar,* "Are you what men say you are?" It is a tragic circumstance that they had to ask. Jesus had done so many things for so many people that his followers should have prepared the hearts of the whole country for him, but they hadn't. I am always amazed at how many people we come in contact with that we can't identify as Christians or non-Christians. We take this for granted, but there are people you meet daily who would like to hear you say that you know who Jesus is. Do you know?

The third speculation about the crowd concerns the wrong answer which was given. This was, "Why, he is Jesus, the prophet from Nazareth of Galilee." It was precisely the wrong answer. At a certain stage in Jesus' ministry this answer would have been all right. At one point many months earlier Jesus had asked his disciples if they knew his identity. They answered that it was the consensus that he was a prophet, and Jesus had not been pleased with this. In that rare moment of light Peter said, "You are the anointed of God, his son." From that time on Jesus was not content with any lesser description. There is a time when being partly right is to be all wrong!

Christ must be taken for what he claimed, or one has no part with him at all. There was a test whose application was recommended by the apostle John because of the many ideas circulating about Jesus at the close of the century, seventy years after his death and resurrection. John said that while we should consider every man's idea, if the man does not claim that Jesus is the unique and anointed Son of God, that man is not of God.

I want to say a word about the councils which were held from the first century through the fourth century. Some of these were heresy trials. There is a reason for this, and the church is not ashamed of them. They were not like the later heresy trials of which the church is ashamed.

Until the fourth century the Christian church did not have a complete collection of data on Jesus. It was only in that century that they assembled documents of the New Testament and began to disseminate them. Previously, all they held out for the common man was the Apostles' Creed or other similar creeds.

Therefore, since the Christians did not have the Bible available in the form it is in now, they had to take strong action to keep men from being misled by powerful and persuasive individuals. When a view of Jesus appeared which was not orthodox, they would condemn it as heresy. And do you know what they used as their guide rule— the few copies of the very books you have now in the New Testament. It was the Bible before it was called the Bible.

Thus, there is no need to have trials today about those things which are now clearly expressed in the Bible. The documents they used then are the same as those in your hand today. The Bible, then, is quite clear about the nature of God, of Jesus, and of man. Any answer about God's or Christ's or man's needs which does not square with the Bible is a wrong answer. You don't need a council, you have a book, and we either believe or disbelieve it. It is that simple. This is why the Apostles' Creed is so important. It kept the early church from going off in the wrong direction. And, if its truth is discarded by the church in this or any other day, that church will not survive and will cease to be a Christian church.

What did Christ claim, and what is there about his claims that is so clear in the Bible? Now, I would admit that there are confusing elements of the Bible but not in this matter. First, Christ claimed that he was the sole mediator between God and man. Second, he claimed a unique relationship with the father. Third, he claimed his own death could make men right with God and that his own resurrection was evidence of his power over death. Herein is the gospel and Paul said "If any man or even an angel from God preach anything less or else, let him be accursed."

All of us are in that Palm Sunday crowd. We struggle with this Jesus, for he touches all men. Does belief in Christ matter? Ask Elizabeth Elliot, wife of a Christian martyr. I can well remember when in 1956 the world was shocked at the news of five missionaries being murdered at the hands of the Auca Indians.

Their exposed film later provided pictures of their first friendly encounter with this tribe. Then something happened and they were killed. But the blood of the martyrs became the seed of the church. Mrs. Elliot, after losing her husband, wrote the book *Through Gates of Splendor*. Recently on network television two of the principal characters on that roll of film appeared, one of whom was one of the killers. The village is Christian now because five men believed so strongly about who Jesus is that they gave up their lives. Ask Elizabeth Elliot, and if you come up with the right answer, you too can know why those martyred young men walked "through gates of splendor."

That first Palm Sunday is important for many reasons, not the least of which is an adequate and satisfying solution to the identity of the lone figure on the donkey's back. The answer one gives determines much more than this world dreams of.

The Plea Christ Would Not Heed

" 'Save yourself, and come down from the cross!' " (Mark 15:30) .

Some years ago a friend of mine described the experience of having been present in the execution chamber during the electrocution of a well-known murderer. Though he had wondered all the week before just what it would be like to observe this act, he was not prepared for one aspect of it—the deep imponderable silence. Said he—"In those moments before death, one has a strange feeling, and it is shared by all the others in the chamber. There is a speechless quiet, bordering on the eerie."

This has not always been the case when men have died. The observers were not quiet when Jesus died. When they saw that he was beyond pulling a miracle of survival from his storehouse of power, they uttered a small word which is translated "Aha." It is an exclamation of scorn. By this little word they were saying—"It's all over now."

Then they hurled one last challenge at him, "If you be the Son of God, *come down from the cross.*" This was precisely the wrong challenge. Jesus had set his face toward this moment, and his death was no accident; he knew what he had to do. I want to mention several ideas which have a bearing on their taunt, "Come down from the cross."

There is first the connotation of derision. This represents the mockers as deriding Jesus. Some answer must be given as to why the taunt was made—perhaps there are several answers.

In the first place, the crowd must have been aware of Jesus' reputation for miracle-working. Perhaps many of them had witnessed some of these miracles. Some of the bystanders could have been like many who are drawn to religious men today—they want to see a demonstration of power, miracle-working power. This fascination of people with religious wonder-workers is no different than that of the man who is drawn to a carnival sideshow. It is highly likely that one segment of the crowd was greatly interested in seeing the miracle of a man who could come down from the cross. In fact, this is one interpretation of the thinking and actions of Judas Iscariot. Some have suggested that Judas, having witnessed many miracles including seeing Lazarus raised from the dead, felt that Jesus would extricate himself.

I know of one man who spends many hours of leisure time checking the ads in the papers for the traveling religious events—whether they are orthodox Christian or not. He truly enjoys the extraordinary things he sees, yet he is not a religious man—certainly not a professing Christian. He would have been among the ones in the crowd who said, "Come down from the cross."

There is another reason the crowd derided Jesus. They were aware of his claim to be uniquely divine. "Are you the Son of God?" said Pilate and Jesus said, "You have said it." There was no criminal guilt in Jesus' case at all; they did not charge him on this account. Yet, they put him to death under the Jewish law against claiming to be divine. *Jesus did not deny his claim.*

There were two distinct ethnic and religious backgrounds represented in the crowd that day. First, there were the Roman soldiers and court officials; secondly, there were the common Jewish people and their religious and civil authorities. Their respective backgrounds entered into the reasons for making the statement, "Come down from the cross if you be the Son of God."

The Romans were well aware of the pagan myths of half-god, half-humans who underwent ceremonies of dying. Although this seems absurd to us, it was not to them. The ancients had their mythological stories that they believed and passed on to their children. But there is a fact worth noting at this point. The Romans had never seen their gods; these gods only existed in their imaginations and in the physical forms of statues and other images. Now, they had come face to face with someone who claimed that he was as much God as man, and this was unsettling.

What had been a religious story in their backgrounds had now become a stark reality. Therefore, they could not accept that a man could be divine and die like a man. "Come down from the cross," the Romans were shouting, and their simplistic reasoning was that if he did not come down, he was certainly not divine.

Basically their reason for not believing in the claims of Jesus is the same reason many men have not believed in him. It is one thing to hear a myth about half-men, half-gods dying, and it is altogether another thing to see it happen before one's eyes. Since that day countless numbers of unbelievers have said that the death of Jesus was the death of a mere man and that all of the church's interpretation concerning his deity amounts to a carry-over from the pagan myths.

Here we see an irony of ironies; the Romans who stood before Jesus wouldn't believe in him, yet they did believe their myths. They had actually believed far more absurd things than they were asked to believe that day. The type of unbelief present then and since then is the same. It is simply this—it is absurd to come to believe that this man was the Son of God.

The second attitude contributing to the derision of Jesus may be traced to the Jews. They derided him for two reasons. First of all, they had misunderstood his words about the temple. Earlier he had said that if "this temple" were destroyed he would raise it in three days. He was referring to the temple of his body and that he would be raised from the dead in three days. They thought that he was talking about their beloved temple in Jerusalem. So they said, "You who would destroy the temple and raise it in three days, save yourself and come down from the cross." It was probably the simple and uneducated in the crowd who said these things. But, there was another group at the cross.

These were the chief priests and scribes. They probably did not misunderstand Jesus in the same way the common folks had. Their taunt had a different slant. They said, "He saved others; himself he cannot save." They were pointing to something far deeper than were either the Romans, who saw a living example of one of their old myths, or the common Jews, who were confused over Jesus' teachings.

The priests and scribes were the religious authorities, and they revealed something far more crucial in their thinking. We remember that they preserved in their tradition several rituals which taught them lessons of God's willingness to forgive their sins. The Jews were keenly aware of sin. They performed a ritual of taking a lamb without spot or blemish and putting it to death as symbolic payment for their sins. They performed a ritual of the scapegoat in which a goat would be abandoned in the wilderness to die symbolically for the sins of the people. Jesus had often talked of being the fulfillment of these ideas. He had called himself the Messiah or the Christ, which meant that he was God's Annointed One. He had talked of saving people and of forgiving their sins. He had even been called the Lamb of God.

It is easy to conclude that these priests were haunted by these images and obviously to some extent under conviction. Listen to their voices, "He saved others; himself he cannot save." Did they concede that he had saved others? They could not have denied the many changed lives about them. Then they said, "Let the Christ, the King of Israel, descend now from the cross, that we may see and believe." See and believe—see and believe—see and believe. How many have followed in the paths of those unbelieving priests—they will *not* see and they will *not* believe. They were requiring God to do something their way if he wished them to see and believe. God did it his way, whether they understood or not. An old gospel hymn tells us, "The way of the Cross leads home." If a man ever comes home to God, he comes by the way of the Cross or he doesn't come home at all.

They told the real truth of the matter. It is not that it would be impossible for a divine being to die (stranger things have happened in this world), but that it is a hard thing to believe. Paul realized this when he went out to preach the Cross; it didn't make good sense, and he said, "To the Gentiles the Cross is utter foolishness, and to the Jews it confuses them so that they fall over the facts." The facts were there for the Jewish priests. In their hearts they knew Jesus was authentic, but they refused to believe. Such was the case of Paul before he was converted.

We have only one conclusion to make. The unbelieving Jews at the cross said it for us although they said it in derision, "He saved others." Jesus is the savior of men—that is the message of the church. You will never understand this message by your reason alone; it will confound you and confuse you.

The Jews were wrong when they said, "Let him come down from the cross that we may see and believe." It is Jesus *on* the cross we are to see and believe. What frame of mind does a man have to possess before he really *sees?* You have to be so convicted of your sins and your need of a personal savior that you are willing to say, "I believe and I commit my heart to you Jesus." How will you know? Even now it could be that the voice of God is telling you that these things are true; but the decision is up to you.

I am thinking of one of the closest friends I ever had. Before I became his pastor he had become a Christian; in fact, even his own pastor did not have anything directly to do with his conversion. Because of his keen training in science for his medical career, he found it hard to rationalize the death of Jesus. The Resurrection, said he, would not be nearly as hard to grasp if he could only grasp why Christ died. He told me that it dawned on him quite suddenly that Christ had died for him, and so he prayed, "God be merciful to me, a sinner for whom Christ died." And suddenly he knew—he knew as no scientist will ever be able to explain. Christ came into his heart. He immediately called his pastor and asked to come before the church on Wednesday to be baptized—not wanting to wait until Sunday.

He was to lose his thirty-seven year-old wife—the mother of his three children—and he would suffer a severe heart attack within the next six years. He would tell you that the healing he found at the Cross sustained him.

We love to sing the hymns of Isaac Watts, and there is one to which later a man named R. E. Hudson wrote the familiar chorus:

> At the cross, at the cross
> Where I first saw the light,

and the burden of my heart rolled away.
It was there by faith I received my sight,
And now I am happy all the day.

Until one experiences this in his heart, he can never know
what Hudson is talking about. Do you know?

The Day Christ Died

"It was now about the sixth hour, and there was darkness over the whole land until the ninth hour, while the sun's light failed; and the curtain of the temple was torn in two. Then Jesus, crying with a loud voice, said, 'Father, into thy hands I commit my spirit!' And having said this he breathed his last. Now when the centurian saw what had taken place, he praised God, and said, 'Certainly that man was innocent!' And all the multitudes who assembled to see the sight, when they saw what had taken place, returned home beating their breasts. And all his acquaintances and the women who had followed him from Galilee stood at a distance and saw these things" (Luke 23:44-49).

This Sunday of all Sundays is the time we think of most seriously about our Lord's passion. I want to speak to you about the day that Jesus died, the Friday after Palm Sunday. The mood of the people can best be described as black, for this was the blackest Friday known to history's chroniclers.

The people of Rome were feverish and restless, partly because of the religious fervor of the Jewish holy season and partly because of the arrest of Jesus. The prince of Rome who occupied the governor's palace was not the only one to capitalize on this restless mood of the masses. The high priest as well as the Jewish king also used this psychological mood to their own advantage.

No really earth shaking deeds are ever accomplished unless the *masses* are swayed. In our century the sight of Hirohito would incite thousands to frenzy. A little-known painter of houses began to make speeches to the jobless working classes. Before long this teeming multitude had transformed him into Adolf Hitler, the Fuerher, and the very sight of this malignant little man set the German people on fire.

For the great English Commonwealth of Nations one man was so eloquent that he literally "spoke" the people to victory. Churchill said, "We shall defend our island, whatever the cost may be, . . . we shall fight in the fields and in the streets, . . . we shall never surrender" (Speech on Dunkirk, House of Commons [June 4, 1940]). Such is the power of individuals to move the people.

That day in Jerusalem was mankind's darkest day partly because of the shouting and inflamed masses who yelled "Let him be crucified." This was the day that Jesus died. No man who has known anything about that day can escape its impact.

What kind of a day was it? The day Jesus died was a day of corruption. The law suffered its worst setback. The Roman law, so beautifully codified, was broken in many ways. Jesus was tried at an illegal hour. He did not have benefit of counsel. His accusers were not investigated. This was the day that Jesus died.

It was a day of political corruption. Pilate laid his duties aside as the fair representative of the empire. He knew that Jesus was innocent and admitted it, but refused to carry out his oath of office. This was the day that Jesus died.

It was a day of religious corruption. The Sanhedrin, the highest council of Jewish religious life, lied. In so doing these men forever sealed the fate of the system of the Jewish priesthood. It had reached an all time low.

When men failed in legal judgment, when men failed in their oath of office, and when men who were religious leaders lied, the day became a midnight of horror.

The day Jesus died was a day of unusual phenomenal happenings. The sun seemingly disappeared for three hours and a horrible darkness came over the land. An earthquake opened graves, and bodies reportedly came to life. People who had been thought dead, though few in number, came forth. The great curtainlike veil in the temple which hid the Holy of Holies was split from top to bottom, and the common man was permitted a view he had never seen before the priests quickly repaired it.

If we grant that the biblical documents are reliable and that they are not later exaggerations of this day, then how does one explain that these very events did not become great evangelistic tools for proving just who Jesus was? Or how is it that the disciples did not rally because of these phenomena? In other words, the early preaching of the apostles in Acts does not incorporate allusions to these events as proof of Christ's deity or as proof of God's activity on Friday. Yet Matthew says they occurred.

How do we explain then that when dead people got up and walked through the streets this did not bring all of Jerusalem to its knees in belief in Christ? Did they not know of this event? Did these other things really happen? If so why was there not some noticeable reaction to these events. Do I believe that these things happened as Matthew describes?

The answer is a resolute yes! The very fact that the people are not described as responding dramatically to these phenomenal events is more reliable than if it had been written that they all became converts. This is more in keeping with man's skepticism. Men have always sinned against truth while claiming they didn't have enough evidence or warning for it. Granting that these things happened—how could it be so and the people fail to respond? I would ask you more pertinent questions.

Where was the widow whose son was raised from the dead? Where were the thousands who witnessed the miraculous production of a food supply from one boy's lunch? Where was old blind Bartimaeus and the others who were healed? Where were the disciples?

All of these people were where you and I have been and maybe where some of us are now—busy trying to explain God out of our lives. We forget his past guidance of our lives, and we become people who talk of belief but practice it little. We are busy looking for excuses not to be committed Christians. Let us not believe that this was the first time man rationalized God out of his universe. This is the game we all play in our personal lives—to doubt, to be pessimistic, to live as we please while justifying our corruption by proving that the higher road is not where life is. Mankind is always one thought away from practical atheism—and that in the face of better evidence to the contrary.

Therefore, for the masses and the disciples *it was not an unusual day because they would not allow it to be.* They did not see these things as unusual until years later. At the time of Christ's death they saw what they wanted to see and overlooked other things on purpose.

Like those disciples who discovered on Sunday that God had never left Jerusalem on Friday, we often wake up slowly to God's presence; in retrospect we see that he has been there in the dark with us all along.

So these things did happen, but every effort was made to pass off the happenings as coincidental to any divine purpose. The disciples were as guilty of passing off these things as were the enemies of Jesus—these things certainly did not rally them on Friday. Perhaps this is how they reasoned. The earthquake was considered rare, but certainly not unheard of. The sun's eclipse was the same. The graves opening was considered common in the sense that people who were not dead had been placed in tombs before. So, that day the events were considered commonplace or, at most, coincidental.

In the book of Acts and in Paul's writings nothing is mentioned about these occurrences, and this has puzzled many readers of the New Testament. Only when the disciples began to reconstruct the life of Jesus did they think of these things, and as they looked back on the day Christ died, they began to put things in perspective. Peter said, "He himself bore our sins in his own body on the tree." The day Christ died he was not thought of in this light, only afterwards.

The answer to the question, "How do men reject such evidence?" is this: We are not ready to accept the activity of God in our lives, so we rob ourselves of the joy of his presence. We are just as guilty of practical unbelief as Jerusalem. The non-Christian will not let God in, and sometimes Christians really doubt if God is around.

It is characteristic of man to pass off God's intervention in his life because he wants God to act in a prescribed pattern. But God works in our lives in his own way. We want some emotional proof or some logical rational proof. God comes to us as he chooses. As the ancient prophets said, God uses emotion and reason for those whose hearts are open. We explain away things like the ones that happened the day Jesus died. I doubt that there is anything that happens to us that does not have a purpose. We leave out the dimension of God so habitually in our lives that we are guilty of great sin before we wake up!

How sad that we have to experience those days of denial and suffering like Peter or outright forsaking of the church as did the disciples.

The day Jesus died was a most unusual day, and it became more unusual the farther one got away from it. It did not have to be that way. If the apostles had remained at his side at Calvary, they would not have had to interpret this day in retrospect. They could have saved themselves the despair of those three days. There is no such thing as a day without God—if we want him. There is a great song that goes, "My Lord, what a mourning, when the sun refused to shine." It was written years later, in retrospect. It is a pity that the first disciples could not have viewed that day in that marvelous light.

What kind of day was it finally? It was a day that changed history. More songs have been composed, more paintings painted, more poetry written, and more thought given to that day than any other day in the whole history of mankind. That day has a strange way of lodging itself in the life of each of us. It is the day that Jesus died. The prophets thought of it and Simon Peter reflected on it in these words, "The Lord of glory was crucified."

All Christians can say with Isaac Watts:

> Alas, and did my Savior bleed,
> And did my Sovereign die?
> Would he devote that sacred head
> For sinners such as I?
> Was it for crimes that I have done,
> He groaned upon the tree?
> Amazing pity!
> Grace unknown!
> And love beyond degree!
> Well might the sun in darkness hide,
> And shut his glories in,
> When God the mighty Maker died,
> For man the creature's sin.

The day that Jesus died was dark, but it has brought more light and vision than any other day we shall ever know.

A Ransom for Many

"Even as the Son of man came not to be served but to serve, and to give his life as a ransom for many. (Matt. 20:28).

Twenty-one years ago a beady-eyed little four-year-old beauty sat in front of the television with a type of hat on her head that at that moment was being worn by hundreds of thousands of other children. She was the child of my philosophy of religion professor, and I would often see her with that Mickey Mouse hat. She would sit on the floor and sing joyously at the beginning of the show. Then when it was time to say good-bye, she would sing the "Mickey Mouse" tune slowly and almost always sniffle at the dread thought of saying good-bye.

An article in the paper recently reported the revival of this Walt Disney show in living rooms and dens across America, only now the daughters and sons of the children of the early fifties are sitting on the floor. I wouldn't be surprised if many of the mothers and fathers are right there with them singing the same songs. Mr. Disney had a way with children. I remember when one of his daughters wrote an article entitled, "My Father, Walt Disney." He had the fascinating ability to speak a language of endless relevance to children.

Now "relevance" is an overused word in many quarters. I suppose in the church we have talked so much about being relevant that we have become boring. Yet, the church has always had the problem and the challenge of keeping up to date. This is especially difficult because our subject matter is essentially founded on a first century document, and it is difficult to create a practical blend of the contemporary and the historical.

One of the charges against the churches and their preachers who were "with it" in the sixties was that they were so with it that they left it. Current events can be interesting, but they can also be tiresome as moldy history. I suppose if beauty is in the eye of the beholder, so is relevance.

Bishop Wheatley in his memoirs of his days at Drew University tells about an experience with dour old Dean Lynn Harold Hough. One day as Dean Hough was calling the roll he got to the name of Harry Robinson. Harry was not there; so, hoping to make Harry's absence seem a little more justified, one of his pals spoke up in his defense. "Dean, Harry can't be here today. You see, he's getting married." To which the Dean soberly replied, "Interesting, but irrelevant."

We are rapidly approaching Easter and this holy season is a very significant time of the year for Christians. Standing before officiating clergy all over the world today are people just like you. There are the first graders and the seniors; there are those with as much education as can be gotten and those with far less than that. There are the rich, the poor, and the vast middle class. Unlike other focal points which divide people into interest groups and educational levels, religion draws its adherents from every level.

There is a question that needs to be asked of all Christians, "Why do you still believe in the Cross?" I suppose that that is the focal point of relevancy for all of us today. If we have anything at all in common, it is a central belief in the Cross. From the first century the cross has been on the altars of churches for all to see upon entering. It is the symbolism which the Cross reveals which unites our hearts. While even the Bible can divide men when they disagree on its interpretation, the Cross has from the beginning united Christians. Today I want us to think about this unifying Cross.

I believe the most beautiful statement Christ ever made concerned his cross. He said, "The Son of man came to be a servant and to give his life a ransom for many." Of all the statements about the Cross, this is the most graphic to me—"[He] gave his life as a ransom for many."

The origin of the word "ransom" is interesting. The word itself means "payment," and it was used in the ancient world to denote huge sums of money. Kings would play deadly games of kidnapping in which they would kidnap important people from the realm of another sovereign. Then a message was sent to ask for a sizeable amount of wealth, either money or goods, in exchange for the hostage's life.

In our day we are seeing this horrible crime of kidnapping for money accelerated. Almost monthly some notable person is abducted, and a ransom note is sent to those whose wealth is to be exploited. As has been true with the church's teachings in so many areas, conflicts have developed that have caused even this simple statement of Jesus' to lose much of its beauty. Let me show you how it has happened.

After the New Testament was put into the form we now know, scholars studied the books in monasteries all over the world. One day, a notable scholar and a prince among the church's intellects was reading this passage and asked a simple question. His question was, "To whom was a ransom paid?" Thus, instead of allowing our Lord to simply pick out a word from the world's vocabulary and borrow its immediate sense, this churchman claimed a more complex significance for the statement overall. He concluded that the payment was made to *someone*, as was true of all ransoms; and the subsequent question "to whom" instigated the famous speculations we now know as the theories of atonement. On the cross Christ made what is called "atonement" for our sins. This word means "to be made one with God." The "how" of this was connected to the "to whom" the payment was made. This opened the door for endless speculation.

There are at least five classic theories of the atonement. One said that Jesus paid the devil off or that the ransom was delivered to him. Other theories were more farfetched and complicated. A study of each of these is interesting, but not important for our consideration at this time.

Let me say that I think that the word "ransom" should be understood as a simple figure of speech. I have a quarrel with much of this historical theorizing. Although all divinity students should be exposed to them, I really think the theories miss the point. I don't believe Christ ever intended that we extend this figure of speech so far.

Here is what I think he meant. I think he was saying that a great price had to be paid for man's deliverance from sin. I think that it was a simple reference to his horrible death which he knew by this time would take place. Here is the mystery of his love. I don't know why Christ had to die for us. I only know that he did. Also, I know that sin takes its toll in human life and that the cost in destroyed values, destroyed goals, destroyed homes, and wars as a result of man's greed and all the other crimes of humanity is included in this toll. If man's sins can account for such cost, it is then easier to see that man's redemption came at no small price.

I don't think that Christ meant us to take this word *ransom* and run off in all directions. It was simply a statement that issued from the pathos of his heart. If a great price had to be paid, a great need had to be present. Probably at no other time in the life of Israel was the nation more aware of sin. It had its elaborate rituals whereby the Jewish priests would absolve the people from their sins. Surely the people sat in darkness and needed to see a great light.

This leads me to the observation that the one word used today by many people who are crying out for help is *trapped*. People feel trapped. Don't ask me to explain it; I can't. It is a universal feeling. One can be trapped by any number of things or ways of life. I do know that when Christ died on the cross, he paid a great price for people who were greatly trapped.

I come quickly to the main thrust of this simple message. This is: if a great price is to be paid and a great need is to be felt, then a great experience is to be had. By experience I do not mean a one-time event. I mean an acceptance of Christ's death for us and a continual experience of contemplation. The gospel signifies that we as sinners must receive this truth in our hearts. Through childlike trust we must believe with all our minds that mysteriously enough his death will set us free just like ransom sets free. But first, you and I have to accept Christ as our Lord and Savior. There has to be a beginning—you are not born with this belief; you have to exercise your free choice.

Let me explain at least one way that when we do become Christian, this wonderful Cross continues to set us free. I can't explain it, but like medicine for the body, when the Christian *contemplates* the Cross, wondrously liberating and purifying things happen to one's heart. You don't have to go around thinking about it all of the time. Yet, when you are disheartened and feel life's troubles strangling you, a hymn about the Cross will lift your spirit. Contemplation of the Cross is healing, mysterious healing.

The Cross unifies Christians, and our worship in the

Christian Church is greatly enriched by having members of other denominations in constant attendance. Some things can't be adequately put into words—such is the Cross and its unifying power.

Elton Trueblood is a Quaker, the most famous of our time. The first day he visited here last Fall, he asked to see the sanctuary. When we walked in he sat down in the first pew and was quiet. We sat there for fully a minute when he said, "This is his house and I am continually reminded that I can only be as near to him as I can think his thoughts." We sat there for several minutes and he talked of his seventy-five years as a believing Christian.

I often think of Charles Wesley's words:

> Jesus! the name that charms our fears.
> That bids our sorrows cease,
> 'Tis music in the sinners' ears,
> 'Tis life, and health, and peace.

We can't all be as great as Trueblood or Wesley, but we all have one thought in common that we hold dear and that is the Cross and all it means.

FOR EASTERTIDE

The Light of His Resurrection

Jesus in the Shadows

"But Mary stood weeping outside the tomb, and as she wept she stooped to look into the tomb; and she saw two angels in white, sitting where the body of Jesus had lain, one at the head and one at the feet. They said to her, 'Woman, why are you weeping?' She said to them, 'Because they have taken away my Lord, and I do not know where they have laid him.' Saying this, she turned round and saw Jesus standing, but did not know that it was Jesus. Jesus said to her, 'Woman, why are you weeping? Whom do you seek?' Supposing him to be the gardener, she said to him. 'Sir, if you have carried him away, tell me where you have laid him, and I will take him away.' Jesus said to her, 'Mary.' She turned and said to him in Hebrew, 'Rab-bo'ni!' (which means Teacher). Jesus said to her, 'Do not hold me, for I have not yet ascended to the Father; but go to my brethren and say to them, I am ascending to my Father and your Father, to my God and your God.' Mary Mag'dalene went and said to the disciples, 'I have seen the Lord'; and she told them that he had said these things to her" (John 20:11-18).

There is something about the period of time just before dawn which is remarkably unlike any other part of the day. Shadows have a beauty of their own. The only difference in the shadows of the early morning and those at dusk is that the late evening shadows grow darker and the early morning shadows fade away. There is a note of awakening as the shadows of the morning give way to the beaming rays of sunlight.

That awful Friday in Jerusalem is like an evening shadow. The events of the day grew darker and darker, and finally the sun itself refused to shine. However as the shadows of Friday meant death, the early morning shadows of the following Sunday gave way to hope in the resurrection of our Lord.

The garden of Jesus' tomb was obviously quiet and beautiful in those early morning hours. Mary was not aware at first of Jesus' identity. Then she became the first to be convinced of the resurrection. But this comes to her hearing and not her sight. She hears Christ's voice as he calls her name. Jesus said to her, "Mary," she turned and said to Him, "Rab-bo'ni." She was glad to quickly respond with the word "Master." I would like to mention a few things about this worth pondering.

There was no living Lord in her mind as she began her journey to the tomb. The exposition by Arthur John Gossip in volume 8, page 792 of *The Interpreter's Bible* contains a beautiful treatment and story concerning this thought.

And many keep making that same mistake, with vast loss to themselves. The Christ they know lived in Palestine nineteen hundred years ago. The record of what he did and taught and suffered moves and impresses them. In thought they often take their stand on Calvary with a very real emotion in their hearts and a new inspiration surging up in them. But they have no experience of the risen Lord, do not walk with him day by day. And that means that their faith, genuine enough and really effective as far as it goes, is something greatly less than Christianity.

R. W. Dale of Birmingham was well on in life and a distinguished leader in the church, of widespread authority, when one day, writing an Easter sermon, "the thought of the risen Lord broke in upon him as it had never done before. 'Christ is alive,' I said to myself; 'alive!' and then I paused;— 'alive!' and then I paused again; 'alive!' Can that really be true? living as real as I myself am? I got up and walked about repeating 'Christ is living' 'Christ is living!' It was to me a new discovery. I thought that all along I had believed it; but not until that moment did I feel sure about it. I then said 'My people shall know it; I shall preach about it again and again until they believe it as I do now.' Then began the custom of singing in Carr's Lane on every Sunday morning an Easter hymn."

Secondly, Mary Magdalene had already once been found by the Lord. No one knew better than she that a person can once be lost and then be found. Though she went in search of Christ, a few months prior to this he had found her in the bondage of sin. It only seems accurate for the total picture that on this lovely, quiet day Mary Magdalene should be the one in search of her Lord. In fact, when she thought he was taken to another burial plot, she wanted desperately to go there. She could not throw off the spell of the one who had found her. Now she must locate him. But, ironically enough, Jesus found her again. This time she was wandering around in a daze of grief.

This is the way it sometimes happens with us. We are surely found in that we have become God's people by commitment and declaration. Yet, through toils and snares, we sometimes need him to find us again. Jesus again found Mary.

Thirdly, although Mary wanted to find Christ, she was not prepared to find him in this new role. She desired to take up where they had left off. He was merely her teacher or Rabbi. Jesus forbade this and told her so. Up until this time his followers had called him Rabbi. He tells her to hold him not. He has a new relationship with all of them. He is now the risen Lord. Actually, she was doing more than touching him. She was holding on to him. He used this embrace as a figure of speech. This is a difficult lesson for us to learn. It was for Mary. Jesus had fulfilled his role as teacher: he had taught his disciples what he wanted them to know. He is now her Lord. She is to follow him. He has led the way as a teacher, but she is not to hold on to him in this old relationship. This is the lesson we all need. We are slow in letting him be Lord and Master in order that we may live for him. There are many who are committed to his teachings but not to his will.

Finally, we see Jesus standing in the early morning shadows, waiting for someone to take him at his word. He said he would not be in that tomb on the third day, and no one was there to believe him except this one woman, and she was uncertain. Jesus may be in the shadows of your life, but he will not step from them unless you make him Lord. All too often many of us have a shadowy relationship with our Lord. We are at that hazy, foggy state of noncommitment. One of the seven churches of Asia Minor was so lukewarm that it was ineffective as an agent for Christian change. The most miserable Christian position is one which reflects only near commitment—never the true light of declaration, always the indefiniteness of a shadow.

All through his short life, Henry Francis Lyte wanted to be a writer. So, on September 4, 1847, his fifty-fourth year, he finished a poem he had begun many years earlier and set forth on his final and fatal journey. Life had been a hard taskmaster to Lyte. He had been very poor, but he managed to complete his training for the ministry, receive Holy Orders, and settle down at the age of twenty-one in a small parish. He had many doubts even yet. He came to write these famous words after being with a dying brother minister.

Jesus, I my cross have taken,
All to leave and follow thee;
Destitute, despised, forsaken,
Thou, from hence, my all shalt be.

By no stretch of the imagination could he be called a successful pastor. His congregation tired of him because he was sick much of the time. After staying twenty-four years in one church the discontent became so bad that he resigned to go away in hope of getting well.

Before he left his final parish in Devon, England, he finished the hymn we call "Abide With Me." He was to die in two months near Nice, France. His last words reflected his continual thought of death. He is reported to have said at the end, "Oh, there is nothing terrible in death. Jesus steps down into the grave before me, and I have both peace and hope."

On his gravestone are engraved these words.

Heaven's morning breaks, and earth's vain shadows flee
In life, in death, O Lord. Abide with me.

In an earlier poem he said, "Grant me, swanlike, my last breath to spend, in songs that may not die." This has happened and we are to sing "Abide with Me" at this time. In this light it is a fitting Easter hymn.

Our Link with Infinity

"But on the first day of the week, at early dawn, they went to the tomb, taking the spices which they had prepared. And they found the stone rolled away from the tomb, but when they went in they did not find the body" (Luke 24:1-3).

The history of man's religious interest has always been centered in his hope that religion would offer him an expectation for life after death. Consequently, each of the world religions has devoted as much time to answering the mystery of the life beyond as it has in offering guidance for the life here.

Basically, religion seeks to do two things. It seeks to mold man's behavior on earth, and it seeks to offer man hope for the hereafter. The Christian faith is no different. The New Testament speaks of our pattern of life on earth and our hope for the hereafter. If all that religion does for man is to offer him help for now, it is really of no greater value than any good human course of life. Lofty and noble ideals may be taught by humanistic philosophers who in no way believe in God or an afterlife.

I would have to be honest and say that if the church offered guidance in this life only, it would not hold much appeal for me. We live in the comfortable surroundings of a cultural belief in life after death as seen through the lenses of Christianity. I am grateful for this, but it causes us to take for granted the real impact that Christ's resurrection made on the first-century world.

We have a large crowd in church today to celebrate belief in the Resurrection. Did you know that the largest crowd which celebrated his resurrection before he went back to heaven was about five hundred people? That was five hundred out of the entire world, and we have that many in this one church today. The day is more and more quickly coming upon us when our culture will require us as Christians to prove that our religion is superior as best we can.

We cannot force the Scriptures upon them when they are not willing to accept it. The early church went out to preach the Resurrection fully thirty years before they were writing what we know as Scripture. Head on, they met a world which said, "We will believe if you can give us reasons for doing so."

What then did the early preachers say? They went out and proclaimed that Jesus of Nazareth was alive and that he had overcome death. Their god had waged war with death, and he had triumphed. Their first message was not how to live good lives here; it was "In Christ, we have solved the riddle of the universe."

I would like to suggest to you today the basic solutions the Resurrection offered for men. In my own pilgrimage it is the Resurrection which offers me the final proof for belief. You must remember that it was not belief in the life of Jesus or his death that changed the world—it was belief in his resurrection.

First of all, the Resurrection made belief in God tangible. By tangible, I mean that one could touch this belief. I'll show you what I mean. Men have from the beginning come forth with arguments to prove the existence of God. There is, to cite just one, the argument from natural evidence. This usually talks about how only God could make a snowflake or a flower or any other natural wonder. Now for those who already believe in God, it is quite easy to assimilate this mind-set. Yet, in the ancient world, order in the universe was not a fact as it is for us today. We now know many secrets which help us to control nature. They did not have such help in Jesus' day.

Even with all of our ingenuity, every year disastrous tornadoes trigger rashes of bitterness, and many people become atheists because of them. In our sermons and from our sheltered experiences, we usually hear of people who become believers in God because of some wonderful effect of nature. Seldom do we hear of those who are turned away by nature. To them, nature's holocausts do not speak of God—in fact, they speak loudly and clearly of ungodliness.

I am saying that there are as many arguments against belief in God from natural evidence as there are for belief in God. The early church did not go out into a world terrified of nature and say "Let us believe in God because of the orderliness of the universe." They would have been laughed out of the cities.

The strongest argument for belief in any position is its link with human experience. If you can touch it, you can believe in it; if you can see it you can grasp its truth. The early Christians reversed much of the logic of belief. The Jews as well as much of the world said, "We believe in God, but we don't believe in Christ." The early Christians said, "We believe in Christ, and because of him we know that there is a God." They reversed it!

Even today men say that they believe in God but not in Christ. I must say to you that my position is the same as that of the early church. It is because I believe in Christ that I believe in God. As I read philosophy and observe senseless death, suffering, and worldwide trauma, I don't find any good reason to believe in God except for Christ. If I did not believe in Christ, I could not believe in God.

This is the position of the New Testament, although we have taken it for granted.

The early preachers went forth saying, "We have seen Christ, and he has shown us God." Listen carefully to St. John as he argues for belief in God because he believes in Christ and has touched him.

Listen to the first letter of John:

> That which was from the beginning, which we have heard, which we have seen with our eyes, which we have looked upon and touched with our hands, concerning the word of life—the life was made manifest, and we saw it, and testify to it, and proclaim to you the eternal life which was with the Father and was made manifest to us—that which we have seen and heard we proclaim also to you, so that you may have fellowship with us; and our fellowship is with the Father and with his Son Jesus Christ. And we are writing this that your joy may be complete. (I John 1:1-4)

The Resurrection made belief in God tangible. It took it out of the argumentative category in which one maintains that there was a God either because of the evidence of nature or the necessity of a first cause. The early church believed in God because they had seen and touched Christ. The Resurrection made belief in God tangible.

Secondly, the Resurrection answers the problem of life after death. Until Christ, the world had drifted along with a hazy grasp of belief in immortality. The philosophers of Greece had argued for a life following this one, and their arguments were beautiful and quite logical. However, at best, one found belief in life after death through faith, surely not through reason.

Yet, the absolute sounds of death's silence kept saying "How do you know you are to live again!" The grave silently screamed "Where is your logic? Where is your proof? I am conqueror." With all of man's faith that he would live again, the grave said, "Where is your proof now." The Resurrection shattered the stillness of the grave. Death and the grave were beaten and subdued at last. We talk a lot about faith. We speak of having faith that we shall live again. Did you know that this was not the approach of the early church? The early church did not go forth preaching that they had faith in life after death. They went forth preaching that they knew they were to live again. There was no faith involved.

The set of their minds was what we would now call scientific. When scientists isolate a germ they no longer say, "We speculate that this is the cause." Instead, they say, "Now we are sure." That is the way the apostles went forth to preach Christ. It was this scientific and absolute certainty that caused men to listen to them.

We look back and say, "I have faith in Christ." They said "We know these things are true." They believed in life after death as much as they believed in life before death. Death was merely the way they got to the other world. It was powerless to frighten them. We talk about faith; they talked about fact. It is at this point that we have missed the message. We are always trying to build faith, and this is well and good, but it excites me to know that this was not the way they preached the Resurrection. They preached fact, not faith! Listen to Peter as he says, "Blessed be the God and Father of our Lord Jesus Christ! By his great mercy we have been born anew to a living hope through the resurrection of Jesus Christ from the dead" (I Peter 1:3-4).

The Resurrection did not give them a good feeling that said they would live again. No! The Resurrection gave them positive proof that as they took hold of a man who was legally dead, that man was now alive. Paul was saying

"We now have a hope which is alive, a lively hope." He means it is based now on fact not feeling. They didn't live by faith—they lived by fact. This is a revolutionary concept and a world away from our feeble whimpering and sighing. The Resurrection answers the problem of life after death.

Thirdly, the Resurrection gave a solution to the infinity of the universe. Where did God come from? What is behind God? Can there be anything on the other side of God? What is out there beyond our experience? These are terrifying thoughts. They send our minds spinning like a top out of control. The Resurrection stopped minds from spinning for all time. Though the early Christians could not grasp all there was to the meaning of the universe, they knew they had met a man from outer space. That is exactly the way they looked upon Jesus. Our minds have romantic ways of stopping at the manger in Bethlehem but theirs did not.

There is great speculation today as to what we would do if spacemen visited us. It would change our view of many things we say. Well, that is exactly what happened to those early disciples. Christ was a visitor from outer space. Listen to St. John as he says of Christ, "He was in the beginning with God." No talk of Bethlehem here. When they touched Jesus they were holding on to a link with infinity.

So the Resurrection gave them the answer to belief in God, belief in immortality, and it pieced together their universe. They remembered when from a mountain top he ascended into the space of heaven and he said, "I am coming back." They had a friend in heaven whom they had touched before he went away. I see men and women touch their dead loved ones before they close the casket. This is their way of touching the world beyond. When Christ went up out of their midst they saw themselves being linked with infinity, and infinity no longer frightened them.

In my college days I heard a noted chemist speak. He was an old man and has been dead for many years now. Brought up in Europe, he was taught by his atheistic parents to be a free thinker. He set out to find the best religion with the most proof. He visited the shrines of Muhammad, Buddha, and Confucius. He listened to the most noted theologians in the world speak on these things.

Finally, he went to Jerusalem and spent a week. He walked where Jesus walked, and he was not moved. He listened to Jesus' words on good living, and he was not moved. But one beautiful day he sat on the Mount of Olives, and the thrust of Christianity hit him as never before. "These people," he said, "were always pointing me to an empty tomb. I had visited the great tombs of the other religions and this was the only empty one I found. From this proven fact, I came to believe in God, in life after death, and I no longer feared the vastness of it all. They kept talking about an empty tomb."

Christianity can be summed up in one great line of thought—talk of an empty tomb. It is our link with whatever else there is.

The Transformation of a Day

"But on the first day of the week, at early dawn, they went to the tomb, taking the spices which they had prepared. And they found the stone rolled away from the tomb, but when they went in they did not find the body. While they were perplexed about this, behold, two men stood by them in dazzling apparel; and as they were frightened and bowed their faces to the ground the men said to them, 'Why do you seek the living among the dead? Remember how he told you, while he was still in Galilee, that the Son of man must be delivered into the hands of sinful men, and be crucified, and on the third day rise.' And they remembered his words, and returning from the tomb they told all this to the eleven and to all the rest. Now it was Mary Mag'dalene and Jo-an'na and Mary, the mother of James and the other women with them who told this to the apostles; but these words seemed to them an idle tale, and they did not believe them" (Luke 24:1-11).

When we are born into this world of people, ideas, and settings, we become the recipients of many customs we often take for granted. One of these customs is the universal celebration of Easter Sunday. It is my favorite Sunday of the year.

It was not always this way. All of the trappings and thought-provoking moods of this day have come about because of a certain event. Before that event, Sunday was marked by only one distinction. It was the first day of a new seven-day cycle and it followed the Jewish sabbath of Saturday.

Stop for a minute and let your mind touch on the significance of Sunday—not just Easter Sunday—but Sunday. It is, as we say, mind boggling. Just think of the alteration of mankind's life because of that first Easter Sunday event.

Not only Sunday but the world was transformed. Think of our political life. The most serious negotiations are usually not held on Sunday. The world of commerce slows to a snail's space on Sunday. Educational institutions resemble ghost dwellings. City streets resemble deserted movie sets.

People are seldom buried on Sunday. In fact, more are born than are buried on Sunday. Hospitals have fewer bed patients on Sunday. In fact, people will overlook illnesses on Sunday and allow them to surface on Monday. People get sick less on Sunday than any other day, that is, except for us ministers who are either ill from our sermons or from looking at empty pews. Trials are not held on that day.

You can't borrow money on Sunday, and you can spend less on that day than any other. I could go on and on. However, in the first century, the first day of the week (as expressed in the preceding scripture) was just that and that alone—just another day—until it was transformed by an event.

In contrast, Friday, the day of the Crucifixion, is seldom given much thought—with the lone exception of Good Friday. Even though more thought has been given to Jesus' death than to his resurrection, that is in poems, songs, paintings, it is Sunday which has become the transformed day. It has never been the same since Christ transformed it and gave it meaning.

The reason is twofold. First is the respect for the Christian celebration of Christ's resurrection. The second is the

custom begun by the Roman government when it proclaimed that this day was to be a day of respect for the
Christian religion. Yet, the latter is not a really good reason.
We don't pay too much attention to some of the other
customs of the Romans or of antiquity in general, as far
as that goes. Thus we are met with the amazing fact that
the first day took on a new meaning.

*This is a new meaning which has not let the world out
of its grasp.* As I said, Sunday was at first significant only
in that it started the weekly cycle over again. It was no
different from the second day, Monday, or the third day,
Tuesday. This is why the only significance the Gospel
writer could attach to it was "early on the first day they
came to the tomb." In fact, the days were not even named
until later. To the Jews they were known only as first,
second, and third days, etc., the seventh being called the
sabbath.

After that first Easter the early church borrowed the
principles of Moses' sabbath—that is to worship, to gather
into groups, and to reflect on their faith. They recommitted
themselves each first day. Quite soon and before they began
to refer to the first day as Sunday like the Romans, they
began to call it the *Lord's day* (as it is still affectionately
known by Christians today).

Sunday now does more than begin the seven-day cycle,
it stands as a silent witness to the resurrection of Jesus. The
first day, so insignificant to mankind, came alive with new
meaning that morning. If the angels could have spoken in
cartoon animation, they would have said "Little first day,
wake up, you will never be the same again and neither will
the world." Pity the Mondays through Saturdays. They
have no significance at all when compared to the trans-
formation of the first day.

*This, then, is a reminder that there is really no intrinsic
meaning for the word "day" except that it be marked by*

activity distinguishing it from other days. Time is really nothing more than a cycling of the sun. We can only remember time by events, not by days. Our lives are really not made up of days but of events. We remember days only because of an event which transformed them from the accumulated tickings of a clock to a momentous occasion.

Like the millions of Sundays before the Resurrection, our days are for the most part indistinguishable from one another. In fact, if an event is not really instrumental in changing our lifestyle or mood, most of us are likely to refer to the past with the statement, "I can't remember what day it was; I do vaguely remember the event." Then there are circumstances that cause us to say, "I can remember that it was on a Tuesday night . . .—I shall never forget it." But, what is significant for your particular sun cycle is not necessarily significant for others. Now and then, however, some event does touch a great many people —just like Easter. I found a clipping in my files I would like to pass on.

PEARL HARBOR REMEMBERED

Pearl Harbor, Hawaii (AP) An oil slick catches the rays of the subtropical sun, expanding in a rainbow of color on the water's surface.

A garland of brilliant flowers joins the widening kaleidoscope.

A gray U.S. destroyer moves quietly through the water, its crew lining the rails, staring at Ford Island on this quiet Monday morning in December.

The place is Pearl Harbor; the time, the present.

The oil slick is from a sunken battleship; the flowers from an anonymous mourner who makes an annual pilgrimage to Pearl Harbor at this time each year.

The harbor is a serene scene, with the mountains of Oahu a backdrop for the blue water.

But 23 years ago today, a few minutes before 8 A.M., hell broke loose at Pearl and in 110 minutes, more than 2,000

Americans were dead or dying; another 1,700 were injured; 8 battleships were sunk or disabled; 4 others were less damaged; and other smaller vessels were damaged, sunk or sinking.

Today is "Pearl Harbor Day."

Members of veterans' organizations visit the white memorial which straddles the sunken battleship Arizona. Wreaths are placed in the chapel, prayers said.

Arriving quietly in ones and twos for the Navy-provided shuttleboat are some whose sons or husbands were among the 1,102 men still entombed in the Arizona.

You can still see parts of the rusted superstructure jutting from the water. Occasionally, oil still bubbles to the surface from the old ship.

The U.S. flag flies over her, signifying the USS ARIZONA remains a commissioned vessel of the fleet on this December 7, 23 years after the United States was plunged into World War II.

I noticed that it was torn out of a newspaper and I had failed to date it. But it must have been written in 1964. Yet, when I read it this past week, it seemed timeless. I remembered that Sunday hearing the grown people speak in hushed tones of the sorrow of that day. December 7 has come and gone countless times, but never again will it be just part of the cycling of the sun.

I say to each of us that life is like a day in time. It has no authentic meaning unless it is marked by eventfulness.

Life must be marked by meaning, or it is only the cycling of the sun. Some people are so trapped and bored by routines that they look on important events with a casualness that marks them as insensitive. They remind me of the woman who remarked to her maid, "I'm sorry you're leaving us, Anna, but I'll not stand in the way if you are going to better yourself." "Oh, no, ma'am," said the maid; "I'm just getting married!"

Meaningful existence cannot be seen from the outside.

Edwin Arlington Robinson's poem "Richard Cory" says it beautifully:

> Whenever Richard Cory went down town,
>   We people on the pavement looked at him:
> He was a gentleman from sole to crown,
>   Clean favored, and imperially slim.
>
> And he was always quietly arrayed,
>   And he was always human when he talked;
> But still he fluttered pulses when he said,
>   'Good morning,' and he glittered when he walked.
>
> And he was rich—yes, richer than a king—
>   And admirably schooled in every grace;
> In fine, we thought that he was everything
>   To make us wish that we were in his place.
>
> So on we worked, and waited for the light,
>   And went without the meat, and cursed the bread;
> And Richard Cory, one calm summer night,
>   Went home and put a bullet through his head.

Allow me to make two observations. Our lives are also like weeks in time. Can you imagine a week without Sunday? Suppose you erased the Sundays from your weeks. Now I am not talking about not attending worship. I am talking about how your world would be without Sunday. It is impossible to put our lives into focus without the Sundays. In fact, if we erased Sunday from the calendar as we have known it since that first Easter Sunday, we would have to rewrite man's history and redo his life's routine. It would be quite a job to erase the impact of Sunday from our many-faceted life. Sunday touches each facet.

That is the way it is with the part of you called a soul. Some of us are trying to live out our cycles of the sun as if there were a part of us which didn't need God. Life is pretty much of a mystery—all of a sudden we are here going through our daily cycles. Some people try to prove by their lives that the cycles can be complete without a thought for their part in the Sunday meaning.

You see, you can't wipe out Sunday; it keeps coming around. You can pretend it isn't there, but you have to pretend for twenty-four hours each week because denial doesn't make it so. Even so, no person can pretend he doesn't have a part of him which cries out for God. Mankind in living his life's cycle of events keeps coming around to his need for God just like Sunday keeps coming around. If your life is an endless series of meaningless hours, it is because you don't incorporate the symbol of the "first day" in your cycle. I don't know of a single person who has attempted to live without commitment to God who has not also given evidence that his life was becoming nothing more or less than an endless, meaningless cycle of the clock.

As Christ transformed a day in time, so he can transform each of our lives. The Christian gospel does more than direct us to heaven; it is seasoning for what can otherwise become a boring procession of the sun.

I often think of Stuart Hamblen and his famous song "It Is No Secret." Hamblen was raised in a West Texas Methodist parsonage, but he tried to prove that his life could know fullness without his father's God. So he set out to deny the need of the symbol of Sunday in his being. He did well—better than most men. He was talented and became wealthy. His life went from Monday to Saturday at a beautiful clip. He was a creature who seemed to prove that man is really a six-day creature.

But, something happened. Don't ask me what, I don't know. He became addicted to alcohol, gambling, and to moral laxity. Now a man need not be like Hamblen to be bored, and I suppose that many people are not slaves to these things, but they still catch that boredom of uneventfulness.

Hamblen attended his first Billy Graham meeting at the suggestion of his wife. After the service one night he asked to see Mr. Graham in his hotel room. Graham told Hamblen he wouldn't find contentment until he could confront the real problem, which was that he was sick of life—totally sick of it.

Hamblen then asked God to come into his life. He meant business. The story goes that one night as Hamblen walked into his home, an antique clock began to chime the strokes of midnight. Inspired, Hamblen sat down and wrote the words and music to a song that was to become the top hit in the nation, a song meant for all those who, like himself, had lost the strength and courage to renew their faith in God and in themselves. To these he promised, "It is no secret what God can do." God could be counted on to pardon them with open arms.

And that's the way it was when Christ transformed the first day of the week, and he's still doing the same thing for those who want their days to be events, not just cycles. Just as Walter Cronkite says, "And that's the way it is [this day, month, and year]," the gospel says, "And that's the way it will always be."

Joyful Reassurance

"And when the sabbath was past, Mary Mag'dalene, and Mary the mother of James, and Salo'me, brought spices, so that they might go and anoint him. And very early on the first day of the week they went to the tomb when the sun had risen. And they were saying to one another, 'Who will roll away the stone for us from the door of the tomb?' And looking up, they saw that the stone was rolled back; for it was very large. And entering the tomb, they saw a young man sitting on the right side, dressed in a white robe; and they were amazed. And he said to them, 'Do not be amazed; you seek Jesus of Nazareth, who was crucified. He has risen, he is not here; see the place where they laid him. But go, tell his disciples and Peter that he is going before you to Galilee, there you will see him, as he told you' " (Mark 16:1-7) .

Equally as important as the Sermon on the Mount or the parables of our Lord are the sayings attributed to him following his resurrection. In an ironic twist of world perspective, these sayings are not emphasized. In fact, most people are not aware of Christ's teachings between the time of his resurrection and his ascension into heaven.

The film industry has proven this point in a classic way. The film *The Greatest Story Ever Told* closes with the Resurrection and the "Hallelujah Chorus." It is as if Jesus never said another thing worth hearing after he returned.

I must say that the four Gospels are not all alike in their records of these sayings. But, that is characteristic of the reporting before the Resurrection as well. Also, if you read the accounts concerning the Resurrection itself, you will notice that each Gospel is different.

According to Mark, a young man is seated inside the cavernous hole where Jesus' body had lain. He tells the women that they should not be frightened because of his presence and because of the absence of Jesus. He then says something that is not recorded in the other Gospels. "Go, tell his disciples and Peter that he will meet them in Galilee." I want to use as our subject, "Go, tell Peter."

Why is this reference to Peter found in Mark's Gospel and not the others. Permit me to speculate. This Gospel is very distinctive in character. It is practically a certainty of scholarship that this Gospel, though written by Mark, was supplied in its detail from Peter. Peter calls Mark "his son" in I Peter 5:13.

The personality of Peter is reflected on almost every page. This is particularly noticeable (some scholars have suggested) in the way the narrative moves so rapidly— almost impulsively—from one subject to another. If it is agreed that the early church was right in ascribing this document to Peter, it stands as a poignant reference to forgiveness. Remember it was Peter who asked how often he should forgive a brother and whom Jesus told "endless times."

It is not unlike Peter to say to the world, "I want you to know how forgiving my Lord was to me." Since the source for Mark's material is Peter, it could be that this statement is included because Peter wanted the world to know for sure that he was forgiven. Now, let us go back to the young man's statement, "Go, tell Peter." I would ask, "Go, tell Peter what?" Obviously the women were to tell Peter that Jesus was alive—that goes without amplification. But, when we read between the lines, we can surely know at least three other things that Jesus was saying to Peter. I marvel at this beautiful action of our risen Lord. He was so concerned about Peter. I think the first thing he was saying is: *Go tell Peter everything is all right between us.*

Can't you imagine the deep sense of guilt Peter must have had? Previously, he had gone on record (without having been asked or singled out personally) as saying that he would be true to Jesus when Jesus announced in the upper room that his followers would forsake him in the hour of trial. Instinctively Simon Peter had responded, "Though the entire world leave you, you can count on me. I would never do such a thing." But, he did! He betrays our Lord by denying that he ever knew him. With an irony never to be forgotten by mankind, Jesus is brought closer to his death by Peter.

What is your life? What is your world? What is human existence? It may be summed up in many ways, but I think one of them is to say that "human life is a relationship of living with people you love and those who love you." Without the relationship of love, existence would be nothing, it seems to me. Your world and my world consist of the relationship of love—those you love and those who love you.

Now think of Peter. He surely was the loneliest person in all Jerusalem on that sabbath day. He had sinned against love. He must have lived in torment. I wonder, don't you, just which one of the women talked to Peter. Because, when the women went bursting in with the news, one of them added that extra message, and it must have gone something like this. "Our Lord is alive and we are to meet him in Galilee, and—oh yes, Peter—the young man in the tomb said to be certain that you got the message."

What a message—everything is all right between us. I

suppose there are no more comforting words in all the world than those heard as children when, despite our unworthy behavior and bitter tears, we heard our parents say "Everything is all right, stop crying."

Go, tell Peter, everything is all right. I know of another thing which was meant by this. Tell Peter, I need him. How good it is to be needed, and how it must have made Peter's heart jump with joy to be needed by the very one he had wronged. This is a reversal of mankind's usual relationship with his gods. From the dawn of early man, men have needed the gods. Now the triumphant, risen Lord indicates that he needs men—especially a sinner like Peter.

But our Lord knew that he needed Peter to be filled with desire to bear the Christian hope rather than with feelings of guilt and inadequacy. He had to start Peter thinking rightly about himself. If Jesus could do this, Peter would become the rock he had predicted he would.

Robert L. Hastings in his work *Hastings' Illustrations* relates the following story:

Angelo Siciliano (popularly known as Charles Atlas, "the world's most perfectly developed man,") was born of Italian immigrant parents in Brooklyn. He grew up in the slums as a scrawny, thin, undernourished lad. At sixteen he weighed only ninety-seven pounds. A pale, nervous runt, he was an easy prey for bullies. Then one day in the lobby of the Brooklyn Museum, he became entranced with the statues of the Greek gods, especially Hercules. He could hardly believe these powerful statues had been posed for by men. So he decided to make himself over in the likeness of a Greek god. He had no fancy gym equipment, but he clipped a series of exercises from a newspaper and devised his own system for tensing one muscle against the other.

It was hard work. Other boys made fun. But he was determined. And eventually the skinny runt from Brooklyn became known as Charles Atlas, described as a man of "true classic physique, in perfect proportions."

If you ever visit the statue of Alexander Hamilton in front of the Treasury Building in Washington, D.C., or the statute of George Washington in the Washington Square monument in New York City, remind yourself that Charles Atlas posed for the sculptor.

The late William James is perhaps best noted for his insight that if a person changes his attitude toward himself, he can actually change himself. Proverbs 23:7 said the same truth centuries ago, "For as he thinketh in his heart, so is he."

"Go, tell Peter, I need him." The third implication of this message is, "Tell Peter the world needs to know what he now knows." The world needs to be constantly reminded that the nature of God is to forgive, not to punish. It is comforting to know that God is more willing to restore the penitent, than to punish the sinner. Someone has said, "The most precious thing about Jesus is the way in which He trusts us on the field of our defeat."

The Resurrection means much but one thing stands out —"No situation, not even death, is greater than our ability through God to overcome." The world needs to know this— that life can be conquered through Christ.

Probably one of the deepest Christian thinkers our generation has known is Karl Barth, the Swiss theologian. In his vintage years, when he was lecturing all over the world, he was asked what was his most profound thought. He replied, "The most profound thought I ever heard was told me by my mother as she sang 'Jesus loves me, this I know, for the Bible tells me so.' "

One of the most prolific of hymnists was Phillip Paul Bliss. He died in a tragic train crash at an early age. The last song he wrote was found in the wreckage and this is part of what it says—

> O if there's only one song I can sing,
> When in His beauty I see the great King,
> This shall my song in eternity be,
> "O what a wonder that Jesus loves me!"

This is a simple thought, a lovely thought, a touching thought. Yet, I think that there has never been in the history of the human race a more revolutionary thought. It made Peter and millions like him new people. It is powerful for changing lives beyond comprehension.

Go, tell Peter the world needs to know what he now knows, and now you and I know it. I'm glad, aren't you?

FOR PENTECOST

The Leadership of His Spirit

Who Is This Holy Spirit?

"Now concerning spiritual gifts, brethren, I do not want you to be uninformed. You know that when you were heathen, you were led astray to dumb idols, however you may have been moved. Therefore I want you to understand that no one speaking by the Spirit of God ever says 'Jesus be cursed!' and no one can say 'Jesus is Lord' except by the Holy Spirit. Now there are varieties of gifts, but the same Spirit, and there are varieties of service, but the same Lord; and there are varieties of working, but it is the same God who inspires them all in every one. To each is given the manifestation of the Spirit for the common good. To one is given through the Spirit the utterance of wisdom, and to another the utterance of knowledge according to the same Spirit, to another faith by the same Spirit, to another gifts of healing, by the one Spirit, to another the working of miracles, to another prophecy, to another the ability to distinguish between spirits, to another various kinds of tongues, to another the interpretation of tongues. All these are inspired by one and the same Spirit, who apportions to each one individually as he wills" (I Cor. 12:1-11).

God the Father, God the Son, God the Holy Spirit. This phrase is well known in the Christian world, for it describes what we know as the Godhead. The early church fathers worked this problem through and came forth with a standard explanation: there is one substance and three manifestations without diminishment of the one. Now, that is difficult to understand, but I can approach it another way. H_2O is the chemical designation for two parts hydrogen and one part oxygen.. This makes water.

Now look upon what we call God's substance as you would H_2O. Then think of H_2O as it is seen in liquid, in ice, or in steam. This is a very quaint way to describe God in three persons, and while it does break down technically, at least the children and I can understand it.

God is one substance, but he is manifest in three different ways. The Latin word *persona* means "mask," and it refers to the masks actors used to change their faces. Therefore, the early bishops in their councils used it to describe God. They called the three persons in one the Three Masks of the Godhead. So when God the Father, God the Son, and God the Holy Spirit were used, they were referred to as *the Godhead*.

The *Holy Spirit* and *Holy Ghost* mean the same thing. The problem is one of language. The synonym for *ghost* or *spirit* is really "breath." A literal translation of the *Holy Spirit* would read the "Holy Breath." *Spirit* was used to indicate nothing more or less than God's actual presence. Let us see it another way. God the Father we have never seen—no man, in fact, has seen God. Therefore, he is God the removed. Then there is the second person, God the Son, and he was touchable—he became a man.

So we have God the removed, and Jesus, God the visible. Then Jesus went back to where he came from, and he said that he sent the Holy Spirit. The Holy Spirit is really the combination of God the Father and God the Son. He is invisible like the Father and we experience him as if the Son were yet present within us. He, then, is God the combined.

We always speak of the Holy Spirit as "he" or "him"

rather than "it." We sense his presence; we can feel him. Now, does this open up problems! The sensation or the interpretation of when his presence is felt has had to be closely determined by proper concepts. The early church put a safeguard on it, and here it is. If you said that an act was caused by the Holy Spirit you had to *measure* it by the other two persons, God the Father and God the Son or else you might not be describing the activity of God at all.

Have you ever had someone say "You did that just like your father or your mother!" The person speaking could have been wrong, or they could have been right. It all depended on how well they *knew* the person referred to.

I know that the Brown family of John Brown University in Arkansas will forgive me for what I am about to say. Since I only met John Brown once, I know nothing more about him than what I have seen and heard. But I have heard enough of small talk and rumor to know that if it were all true, he would have to be schizophrenic. There are people describing him and quoting his views who have never met him.

Now how can we find out if they are right? We can check with those who knew him best—his family and close friends. He cannot have been all the things men have tried to make him to be. This is always true of strong men who cast large shadows.

This is the way it is with understanding the Holy Spirit. Whenever a person claims to be under the power of the Holy Spirit, you judge him by what you know about God and Jesus or, crudely put, by his family, by his substance. The biblical documents and history help us here. But you say, don't all men trace their actions to some parts of the Scriptures? The answer is yes. That is why we need theological education—to treat the Scriptures correctly. The aberrations stem from misinformation. This fact of history is beyond refutation.

Now let us pursue the Spirit in the life of men. Since his presence is unseen yet real, people have done all sorts of things to prove its authenticity.

There has always been the obvious temptation to fabricate acts to prove the presence of the Holy Spirit. For the most part this happens with well-intentioned persons who wish to show that God is at work in their lives. Not all are well intentioned, however. Some are charlatans, as the film documentary *Marjoe* pointed out. If one knows what to look for he can spot manipulation. Sadly enough, lay persons are not trained in religious psychology or in biblical skills, and they often are taken in.

Unfortunately, these so-called Spirit-possessed acts are like firecrackers. The spewing and sputtering of the ignited fuse holds all in its spell until an explosion occurs. When the crisis hits, the person screams, writhes, speaks a strange language, dances, etc., only to collapse in physical exhaustion.

Persons have been known to crawl on the ground, bark like dogs, foam at the mouth, or faint dead away at the touch of the leader. In the last century this was called "being slain by God." In the midst of such occurrences people are decidely thrown beyond the limits of the rational.

Historians know what is at work here. The ancient pagan religion called Gnosticism had many forms. One of them was to suggest that the body, including man's mind, was evil. It said that the soul within man was good. But the soul must be freed from its evil body which was like a jail cell. When the soul was freed the body would convulse and flip around. This was the proof that the good soul inside was shaking the cell doors. When the body passed out, the soul was set free and was joined with the good Spirit above. Of course, it came back home to the body later, to be expulsed all over again.

A Christianized form of Gnosticism said that the Holy Spirit would trouble the good human spirit within persons and help it wage a battle to free it from the body. Thus, unnatural and jerking spasms were proof that the battle was taking place. This belief was common all over the world of the first century. It was rampant in one Christian church in Corinth, Greece. Paul addressed a letter to those at Corinth. He says that he can do all of these things they are reported to be doing. He understands the Oriental mind set for emotional ecstasy. He does not say that God can't work in such an unusual manifestation, but he warns against it.

We could wish that he had taken a firmer stand because that form of Christianized paganism destroyed the church at Corinth, and present day adherents quote him to justify themselves on Christian grounds. To this day a few isolated verses of Paul's implying tolerance have given rise to entire movements.

It is interesting that the Second Person of the Godhead, Jesus, did not speak in tongues or recommend speaking in tongues. One reference in Mark in which Jesus is reported to declare that proof of the Spirit's presence is speaking in tongues is not found in the older Greek manuscripts. In that passage also, Jesus is supposed to have said that proof of being filled with the Holy Spirit is further displayed by handling poisonous snakes and not being bitten, in healing people at random, in chasing demons out of people, and in drinking poison and not being affected by it.

I don't believe that this passage is authentic. Scholars agree it shows signs of having been added much later, during a period of intense superstition. Even the great Greek scholar of the conservative Southern Baptists, A. T. Robertson, said in 1925 in his *Word Pictures in the New Testament* that these are not authentic words of our Lord.

Modern translations tell you this in the footnotes to the last chapter of Mark.

So, all of this philosophy finds its biblical roots in this spurious passage and in the Corinthian letter. Obviously, the idea was pagan and was later Christianized. Also, there is no cop-out for biblical literalists. The Greek construction does not say you *may* prove God's presence by this. It says you *shall;* it is mandatory. Well, it isn't to me. I'm not about to drink poison and handle snakes. And, I'm not going to piously hold the Bible up and say I believe every word as it is stated, because a man believes *what he practices,* and *I don't* practice this.

This is why for the same reason we have schools of medicine, we have theological education—to keep men from making fools of themselves and doing bodily injury. While we were in Nashville, Tennessee some time ago a preacher died after handling a huge snake. The picture of him holding the serpent was on the front page. It was taken a second before he was bitten.

I would rather give my daughters a scalpel and tell them to begin surgery on themselves than give them the Bible and tell them to try to practice every thing that it preaches. There are mandatory skills and guidelines for both activities. When people reject theological education they are guilty of sins against truth. If youths are presented an inconsistent, irrational gospel when they are young, they will spew it out in later years. So, we must measure the work of the Third Person of the Trinity by the first two Persons.

Giving further support to the evidence of a Gnostic influence upon the idea of the Holy Spirit is that the desire for ecstatic and frenzied display to prove union with God is not unique to the Christian religion. It is found in the Orient, especially in the near East. In fact, the so-called spirit-filled demonstrations are seen in greater degree in that part of the world than here. There, it was always called paganism. Also, psychology has shown that these excesses are more apt to surface in unstable people. This is consistent with the idea that some people make better subjects for hypnosis than others.

More importantly, Gnosticism comes into conflict with Christian truth in that it denies the Christian doctrine of Creation. In Genesis God looked on what he had made and called it good. This included the mind. In fact, in Jewish thought the mind was referred to as the center of man's will. Therefore, for a person to become ecstatic (thereby numbing or enchaining his faculties) to prove that God has gotten a hold on him is not a Christian premise. It is pagan to the core. The mind is good; God made it, and to do away with it to prove union with God is absurd. Jesus quoted Moses as saying we should love God with all our minds. Certainly love for God was not to be expressed by drugging the mind with emotions.

There is, then, a proper way for us to perceive the Holy Spirit at work. A close reading of the Pauline text (and we have already answered the one in Mark) says that the Holy Spirit uses us. We don't use him. In mentioning the so-called gifts of the Spirit—tongues, healing, interpreting tongues—Paul says that the Spirit operates as he wills. The Charismatic movement reverses this. They use the Spirit; they bottle him up and even teach courses on how to get him. You can't do this. He gets you; you don't get him. It is absurd to teach a course on how to be filled with the Spirit—how to be used by the Spirit, *yes,* but not how to use him!

The gifts of healing, as well as these other gifts, do not come as a vocational calling. Rather, the Holy Spirit uses persons for healing as he chooses. The word Paul used for healing is plural; *gifts* of healing, not *gift.* There were many ways healing occurred.

It is obvious that the one gift Paul mentions that several

people have exploited is the healer role, and this is not surprising. Poor, maimed, suffering people want to be healed more than they want faith or the other gifts. Thus, this can be a lucrative endeavor if you can convince people you are a tool for men's healing. I know they don't claim to be healers, but they do claim to be a tool, and that is the same thing.

The concrete refutation of this is that these people are God manipulators. How do they know that it is God's will to heal on the night they open their show in town? According to Paul the Holy Spirit puts healing and all of his other characteristics into operation as he wills, not as the sign boards indicate, and not following a notice in the paper that tells us God will begin work tomorrow at say, 7:30 P.M.

I am saying that a professional role founded upon any of these gifts has no scriptural validity. Paul's words are being twisted. Also, the so-called prayer language is absurd. Paul said, "I will pray with the spirit and I will with the mind also." How can you pray with the mind if you don't know what you are saying? Yet, we are now hearing that prayer is more meaningful if it is done in an unknown tongue.

Thus, the conclusion of the matter is that the Holy Spirit must be seen as he is seen in the life of Christ or in the mind of God or in the Old Testament. The Holy Spirit is the presence of God and I ask for his [Holy Spirit] guidance each day, and so should you. He takes our faculties and enhances them, he sharpens our minds and our skills. He does not deny these or throw them into limbo, thus making us do irrational things. To be filled with the Spirit is to be more rational than ever, to be more incisive than ever, to teach the truth better than ever, to develop our skills with Christian dedication. It is to have the breath of the *Godhead* upon your life. It is to be like the Father and the Son.

Unveiling the Father

"And Jesus asked his father, 'How long has he had this?' And he said 'From childhood. And it has often cast him into the fire and into the water, to destroy him; but if you can do anything, have pity on us and help us.' And Jesus said to him, 'If you can! All things are possible to him who believes.' Immediately the father of the child cried out and said, 'I believe; help my unbelief!' " (Mark 9:21-24).

Elton Trueblood once said to me, "I think that the single most significant thing Christians can do when they gather is to affirm their beliefs in a public manner. Don't ever deny the place of a creed in the public assembly." These have been my sentiments for years, and the Apostles' Creed is always used at funerals if I officiate.

One day about ten years ago, I penned the most liberating thought that I had ever had. Do you know of one thought you have had which has come closer to setting you free than any other? Here is mine. The one most liberating thought I ever had was that I did not have to believe in God if I chose not to! I had been in the professional ministry for some fourteen years, and this thought set me free. To the young people let me say, the same can be true with you.

When it was clear to me that I didn't have to believe in God, I was then free to do two things. First, I could stop being on the defensive with avowed atheists and secondly, I could then believe in God because I wanted to.

There was a reason for this startling revelation to me. It was in the way I was reared. I really believe that I can speak for you or for most of you. During World War II, I spent most of my childhood years in a small agricultural-ly-oriented town. It seemed to me that the peerless painter of Americana, Norman Rockwell, used to paint my town every week on the front of *The Saturday Evening Post.* In fact when the *Post* died it hurt me more than the loss of *Life* magazine. I was the freckled faced boy with the cotton top head. We only had eight blocks of the cement road called Main Street and very few streets that were black-topped.

Saturday was the greatest day in the week, as the wagons would come to town making their way down the Main Street to the wagon yard. I can still hear the sound of the wheels on the pavement. All of the cars were from prewar days because no cars had been assembled since then. No one minded if boys jumped on the beds of wagons to ride to the heart of town. The Statler Brothers had a hit song some time ago in which they reminisced about the old Saturday afternoon Westerns. They sang "Whatever happened to Johnny Mack Brown and . . . Lash Larue?" Lash Larue became a Pentecostal preacher, that I know. This is Americana as I remember it, and the pace was as slow as the wagons going into town.

There was Captain Marvel, The Crime Doctor, Charlie Chan, Judy Canova, and others of Rockwell's America. Oh yes, and there was God. His day was the next one after Saturday. Just as I never thought about disbelieving in the essential morality of Gene Autry, the forbidden idea that there was no God never crossed my mind. At the same time, our weekly public assembly in school would find all twelve classes gathered in one auditorium to sing songs about the war, and just as Joel McCrea was always on the side of right, so God was on America's side in the war. We sang

"Praise the Lord and Pass the Ammunition," and the two were synonymous; they meant the same thing.

We sang "Coming in on a Wing and a Prayer," and the prayer was to God, of course. At night we would sometimes tune in the grand lady of song on the radio as she sang our President's favorite, "God Bless America." No one has ever sung it like Kate Smith.

There is the pledge of allegiance which only later used the Lincoln phrase "one nation under God." Instead, we had the word "indivisible," and most of us said "invisible" for a long time. We hardly knew what indivisible meant but our culture did tell us what "under God" meant. The entire culture of Rockwell's America fed the patriotic belief in God. The community dictated that we all believe in God, it was the right thing to do. In fact, we were never asked "did we" but *when* did we wish to confess it publicly." We had no other option.

I remember two men in the community who were supposedly unbelievers. One had a grocery store that was open on Sunday, and this infraction of the sabbath law was a flagrant corroboration of his unbelief. When we heard our ministers preaching against stores being kept open on Sundays, we could only conclude that he was anti-God. Of course, he was a fine man; but it was hard for a young boy to figure out how this could be so if he didn't go to church.

Then there was the church. Our preachers would energetically tackle a man named Ingersol who was supposed to be a threat to belief in God. There was the threat of a dreadful never-ending hell of fire prepared for those who didn't believe in God. Then there was the Bible. It declared that there was a God and almost everyone in our town, believed in the Bible. Do you get the picture? The community, the culture, school, entertainment, peer pressure, and the most powerful voice in our lives, the church, said there was a God. You just naturally signed up for belief in God quite early. We adopted belief in God's existence as easily as we accepted the existence of air.

Do you know that you have never seen air? And it never occurred to you to doubt that there was such a thing as air. You and I have seen the suspended particles of dust and collective microscopic debris, but we have not seen the air. We have seen the leaves blown by the force of the wind, but we have not seen the wind. That is the way it was with believing in God. He was like the air, we never thought of denying either.

All of us have been conditioned, some to lesser, some to greater degrees, to believe in God. Our coins proclaim this, and our lungs breathe it in. Yet, there comes a time when each person wants to either believe, or disbelieve without fear of suffering reprisal. Thousands of people, my kind, your kind, are suffering an erosion of belief in God every day. Why?

I know of one answer—they may never have heard that they didn't have to believe *unless they wanted to*. They have not heard that God doesn't want forced belief. They need to hear that they are free—then they can begin to put the pieces of true belief together.

For a moment let us consider the classic justifications for belief in God. Normally when one seeks to persuade unbelievers to belief, one resorts to some of the classical arguments for God's existence. Now there are some *great* philosophical arguments. One of the most wonderful things I ever learned was that some of the most brilliant persons in history were believers in God. I am glad to belong to the Holy Catholic Church of the ages. If you desire some good logical philosophical support for arguing about whether there is a God or not, I point you to Augustine, Aquinas, and Anselm.

These were not unlearned men, and they are still respected for their philosophical proofs of God. Oh yes, there is the easy way to prove God which is to take a Bible in your hand and ask if people give mental assent to its truths. But, what if they say no? If the Bible is our only proof of God and they say no to its credibility, we have then lost our argument.

I have three personal reasons for my belief in God. First of all, since I am free to choose and God doesn't want me to deny what I feel way down deep, I now believe in God because I want to. I would rather live in a world where God is than where he is not. I respect the philosophical arguments for proving God, but I have spent my last moment indulging in such verbal battles. I would rather turn over and go to sleep. I used to sit up half the night trying to justify belief in God. Now I am quite willing to say to an acknowledged unbeliever, "if that suits you, that suits me, it's your red wagon, so pull it."

When it is all said and done, we all rely on blind, simple trust. There are a lot of reasons to doubt there is a God— but if there is just one, just one to justify belief *in* God, I had rather have my life linked to it. There are only two alternatives about God, either you do believe or you don't. And with no degree of pressure to conform, I believe in God simply because belief weighed against unbelief is better for me.

The second reason I believe in God is that I've lived long enough to observe that people can be like road maps. I keep road maps in my car not to tell me something about the roads I am familiar with, but to guide me in those roads I have not yet traveled. There have been a great number of people who have influenced my life, but I find that those who have best shown me a way over that part of life I have yet to travel have been believers in God.

The way through this life is so crooked that it is easy to get lost. And, it is easier to get lost without God. I have

observed that those who never make it, who destroy themselves, almost always do this in direct proportion to their
distance from God. I can almost assure young people that
the world will many, many times seem one step away from
coming unglued. Those who seem to be able to keep
putting it back together do so through belief in God.
Those who think they can make it without God don't
have a very good track record.

Only a fool begins an uncharted trip without an adequate map! I believe in God because I have been shown
the way by others who made it—not all famous people, but
they finished their course; they did not lose their way.

Last of all, I believe in God because of religious experience. Now what is that? I am not talking about going out
of one's mind to prove that God, as the kids say, "zapped
you." I can explain it this way. Paul said, "God's spirit
touches our spirits and makes us know that we are the
children of God." That is how God talks to us.

I can illustrate religious experience by the feeling one
gets at times when one hears the national anthem. You
may not have been at Fort McHenry but somehow you
know deep inside what went on. It does not always happen,
but there are some moments when you hear the anthem
that you really believe in America simply because of what
you experience in your inner person.

I believe in God because at certain times and in certain
places and under certain conditions he has touched me.
Sometimes when we sing some of the great hymns, I feel
a voice deep within saying, "This is so, this is so." It would
be impossible to deny my inner experience.

My young friends, you will never have to think that you
must rebel against belief in God, if I can impress upon you
that you do not have to believe if you don't want to.

But, the old prophet of Israel said long ago in behalf of

God," "If with all your heart you truly seek me, you shall surely find me, says the Lord." In the freedom to believe or not to believe I recommend the breath of God upon your life. It will make your way easier and your burden lighter.

When We Prevail Over Temptation

"Then the devil took him to the holy city, and set him on the pinnacle of the temple, and said to him, 'If you are the Son of God, throw yourself down; for it is written, "He will give his angels charge of you," and "On their hands they will bear you up, lest you strike your foot against a stone." ' Jesus said to him, 'Again it is written, "You shall not tempt the Lord your God" ' " (Matt. 4:5-7).

If our lives are to be led of the Spirit we must undergo the discipline of temptation as did our Lord. When we consider the written material from which we learn about this part of our Lord's life, we quickly come to the conclusion that much of what we see is autobiographical. This is to say that since no one was with him in the Judean wilderness, only he could have told of his experiences.

We know at least four things about these temptations. First, it is obvious that Jesus used the Scriptures to equip himself with good thoughts for a defense against evil. Second, he rejected a faith which was founded on sensational appeals to God. Third, he endured a period of intense emotional disturbance without the aid of other humans. And fourth, he was personally victorious over the assaults of the evil one.

The word temptation is an interesting word. It can have a twofold aspect. One is to tempt—in the sense of inciting a person to sin. The other is to test—in the sense of trying the strength of a person's character. Actually, the temptation of Jesus took on both aspects. He was tempted to resort to the lowest of motives, as we shall see in a moment. At the same time, he was tested so that he would be prepared for the rigorous ordeal of his future ministry and eventual death.

Greatness—yes, productive living comes from the most terrible of situations. Robert Hastings has pointed out (again in his *Illustrations*) that although it was Robert Koch who proved that diseases are transmitted by germs invisible to the human eye, it was the French chemist Louis Pasteur who discovered how to use weakened microbes to inoculate against all kinds of infectious diseases.

His first successes were with anthrax and chicken cholera. Next he turned to a search for the deadly virus of hydrophobia. But before he could develop a serum of weakened hydrophobia microbes, he must first find and isolate the killer virus.

To do this, it was necessary for Pasteur to experiment with dogs that were mad with rabies. In the lab he would stick his beard within inches of their fangs so as to suck froth into glass tubes. Using these specimens, obtained at such risk of life, he hunted the microbe of hydrophobia.

And succeed he did. But the serum had to be proven. The first subject was a nine-year-old boy by the name of Joseph Meister from Alsace. His mother came crying into Pasteur's laboratory, leading her pitiful, whimpering, scared child, hardly able to walk from the fourteen gashes inflicted by a mad dog. "Save my little boy," she begged. It was the night of July 6, 1885, when Joseph became the first recipient of the weakened microbes of hydrophobia in human history. After fourteen inoculations, the boy went home to Alsace and had never a sign of the dreadful disease.

When there were a dozen other serious diseases whose

microbes had not yet been found, why did Pasteur risk his life to experiment with the deadly hydrophobia?

The answer may be from his childhood. "I have always been haunted," he said, "by the cries of the victims of a mad wolf that came down the street of our town when I was a little boy."

Somehow Jesus was himself to become a different person when he emerged from the horror of his personal temptations. So let us think of this second temptation when Satan suggests that not only Jesus but God himself is to be tested.

Let us look at the Satanic suggestions. Satan decides to do the most unusual of things—he quotes from the Scriptures. Since our Lord had answered the first temptation in this manner, Satan replies, "The Scriptures indicated that 'God will give his angels charge of his authentic son,' so if you are truly the genuine article, throw yourself down from the temple, for you should simply float to a landing." At this point let's ask a good question. Did Christ and Satan transport themselves like Peter Pan to the top of the temple? Or, did this happen in a vision? Most people think that Satan's suggestion was in the form of a vision in Christ's mind, and if he had decided to follow it, he would have walked back to Jerusalem, climbed up to the roof and jumped. The end result is the same, Jesus knew what the tempter meant. The temple was built on Mount Zion. The top of the mountain had been leveled like a plateau. At one corner of the temple, where two porches met, there was a drop of some four hundred and fifty feet into Kedron's Valley.

Malachi, an Old Testament prophet had predicted, "The Lord whom you seek will suddenly come to his temple" (Mal. 3:1). Now, since Satan quoted Psalm 91:11-12, which says that God will protect his Messiah when he comes, and since Jesus knew that Malachi had predicted that God's Son would surprise the nation by coming to the temple, this becomes a real temptation indeed.

Let us see the issue more closely. Christ knew that in order to get the attention of Israel he needed to proclaim his views about God, he had to draw attention to himself. What Satan suggests just might be a good way to begin his ministry. He could prove his trust in God by jumping. Also, by floating down, he could prove to the masses that he was ready to court instant death for his cause. This is drama indeed, and he could have made a real case for his cause—that is if he had lived. Ever since I can remember movies, I can recall seeing priests talking people out of jumping off roof tops. I often wondered what I would do. I got my chance and I didn't like it.

One hot summer afternoon a friend and I were traveling from Greenville, Mississippi, back home to Lake Village, Arkansas. As we followed a slowly moving car to the crest of the huge Mississippi River span, we were finally able to see around the car and to pass it. I looked back because my view on the passenger side revealed that the driver, a woman, had just stopped the car and proceeded to get out. I turned to my friend and told him of my fears. He backed up to within fifty feet or so from her car.

By this time she was over the railing and standing on a utility pipeline practically out of sight. I drew near and said as calmly as I could, "Lady, don't do it! Whatever your problem is, this won't help a thing." After thirty minutes of talking (while the line of traffic grew to a mile in both directions), the drama unfolded at the center of the bridge.

I tried to think of every problem she might have had and eventually spotted a wedding ring on her far hand. Guessing that she might have children, I began to talk of them. Fortunately she had one little girl. As she began to cry, she did not notice that my friend and I—and one other man who had eased up on her other side—were close. At my signal we grabbed her, and after a violent struggle, we pulled her through the railings.

The state police came about this time, and we took her to the hospital where she was treated for shock. Her domestic problems had reached such a stage that she had decided to resort to suicide to prove a point—which she certainly did.

Sometimes people get good intentions confused; and, to make a point, they are tempted to act unwisely. Sometimes to prove love, parents indulge children, and the result is to destroy them. The devil tried to confuse our Lord's mind by suggesting a worthy goal but a bad way to achieve it. I should say here that our Lord did use miraculous powers, but his approach was to carefully select the times, persons, and places for using such powers. Never did he perform miracles as a sideshow artist. Usually, he showed them in out of the way places—with a few notable exceptions.

Thus, let us see his use of Scripture and how it can apply to us. Jesus again quotes from Moses, "You must not put the Lord your God to the test" (Deut. 6:16). Jesus knew that to hazard his life on a passage of scripture was an insult to good sense and to true faith. He knew that if he once began to attract people with sensationalism, he would have to produce even greater wonders to maintain this power. We all know that what is sensational today is commonplace tomorrow. Are you as enthralled with the moon and stars as you once were?

George Buttrick in his exposition of Matthew in volume 7, page 272 of *The Interpreter's Bible* has said concerning this, "Conviction goes deeper than the eyes. God is not proved by sleight of hand: The soul has its own testimony and God is his own interpreter." Thus we must not insult the meaning of faith by regarding God as we do electricity.

Also, with all of the miracle business presently so popular, we should return to the relevant passages and read them carefully in the light of *this* temptation. The "expect a miracle" statement is exactly the same thing that Satan said to Jesus.

This past week a man said to me that his church had literature which urged that people tithe in order to test God's favor. I reminded him that this was the second temptation of our Lord and he said that he and his wife had come to the conclusion that this was bad advice and that if God didn't choose to make them wealthy, they would tithe because it was right to do so. I find it sad that good, conscientious lay persons have to be exposed to so much misguided logic.

There are so many conclusions that can be drawn from our Lord's experience. The best to me is "Don't even do noble things like giving away your money in order to prompt God to do something for you." Victory over temptation comes by following the Holy Spirit's leadership in right conduct one step at a time. I find from our Lord's life that he chose to do what was right and he left the timing of the reward to our Heavenly Father.

David O. Woodyard in his book *Strangers and Exiles: Living by Promises* (Philadelphia: Westminster Press, 1974) tells of a summer day in a remote area when he "found a three-year-old boy rubbing his eyes and sobbing gently. I asked him who he was and where he lived. The only thing he could communicate was his name, Tony. He pointed to his feet, which were bleeding from the stone roads. I picked him up and held him in my arms. After a few minutes I asked, 'Tony, how are we going to find your home?' With renewed confidence and remarkable courage he looked at me and said, 'You just start walking and I'll tell you when we get there.' "

Don't push God—start walking with him, and he'll tell you when you get there. That is what Jesus did in the Judean wilderness. Paul said that God would provide us a way out of temptation if we would be patient in "well doing." The way of escape is the way of service.

Watch Out for the Swine!

Do not give dogs what is holy; and do not throw your pearls before swine, lest they trample them underfoot and turn to attack you" (Matt. 7:6).

We are well aware of the fact that any good teacher warns his students about certain pitfalls in life. Jesus is no exception. All through his ministry he warned of various dangers his followers would face.

Injected between a passage on judgment and a statement on prayer is a little word of warning we can easily pass over if we are not careful. I had preached from the Sermon on the Mount many times before this verse reached out to me. I now believe that it is one of the most fascinating things Jesus has said in all of his ministry.

There were packs of wild scavenger swine as well as dogs in Jesus' day. When a child would go into the woods, his parents would say, "Watch out for the dogs or watch out for the swine!" The swine could attack people—especially children.

Jesus' words are "Do not give dogs what is holy; and do not throw your pearls before swine, lest they trample them underfoot and turn to attack you." A splendid warning, it seems to me, is "Watch Out for the Swine!" He could be talking about many, many things but I'm certain he is talking about our daily routine. *The first thing he seems to be saying is, "Be careful of what you do with valuable things!"*

Why? The lack of care in this regard will render valuables useless. People just did not risk losing a pearl around a pig's pen. Even as water fills up a hole after an object is retrieved from it, so muck and the mire ooze over valuables without any regard for their worth.

All of us have vivid memories of youthful experiences that have served as lessons. As a lad of first-grade vintage, I was sent on an errand for a loaf of bread (which then cost a dime). A summer rain had left mud puddles in the center of small temporary bogs on the dirt street which led from our house to the store.

The admonition not to lose the dime was still ringing in my ears when from my Eden came the sound of the tempter's voice encouraging me to flip the dime above the puddle of clear water and see how many times I could catch it with my eyes closed. The timing was great for a couple of flips, but the third time it fell into the water only to be swallowed up first by the water, then by the sediment beneath.

The calm with which I reached for the dime turned to panic as the water became murky by my search, and for many anxious moments I searched—but to no avail. The dime was useless to me and gone forever as far as my experience was concerned. Of course the climax of the story was rather heated.

Not only would a pearl be lost in the mire of a pigpen but Jesus said that the swine would turn to attack the person who attempted to search for it. Anyone who has kept hogs knows that they aren't always characterized by the "Porky Pig" image. They can be vicious.

We need to go further than the figure Jesus used and see some things which are holy and valuable; some things which can turn on us if they are misused. I am thinking of several. One is time. Time is precious. We can all testify just how fast the years have flown by. Time spent uselessly is gone forever. Time will turn on us. Time is a friend to hold dear but one that refuses our grasp. It is not a slave to any man. Perhaps the greatest common regret is, "I didn't use my time wisely."

Another valuable is knowledge. I am not talking about the accumulation of secular facts such as historical data. I am thinking of a higher level of learning—the knowledge of truth, the knowledge of right and wrong. This is the truth about one's relationship with God, as well as one's grasp of moral values. One can't toy with this because, like swine, it will turn on you. In my counselor's role I once visited a morally depraved girl in a penal institution. When I asked if she knew the difference between right and wrong, she replied, "I did once, but I've rationalized wrong into right for so long that now I really don't know anymore."

Paul mentions that one's conscience can be seared or scarred unless carefully heeded. Also, another of his warnings is in Romans, chapter two. Here he mentions people who in Rome attempted to live as laws unto themselves until they became sexually depraved with absolutely no moral value left in this area at all. He said that the worst thing that befell them was confusion. When any person loses his sense of moral perspective, he can become twisted to the point that black seems white and white seems black. The person who knows what he ought or ought not do but does not heed the voice one day loses the voice. This is the worst state of all. Then the swine turn on him.

Health is another valuable thing. When good habits aren't practiced health can turn on us. There are any number of habits which can cause death. Damage to vital organs is a horrible price to pay for excessive tastes. I have often been by the bedsides of people who have wasted their health; the trampling of the swine is not a pleasant sight.

Our children are gifts from God. The Jews always thought of their children in this way, and the Bible is filled with examples of parents dedicating their children to God. They wanted to tie the life of the child to the church.

I once knew a father who was too busy for his son. Over a two-year period I saw the lad go from bad (which the father did not object to) to worse. Then the father panicked. One day he stopped me at an intersection. While both of us were sitting in our cars, he said these words, "I have lost my boy. He will not have anything to do with me. He just told me that he had no respect for me." That father was being trampled by the swine. He had somehow momentarily and maybe eternally lost a pearl in the mire. "Watch out for the swine" would be the message that man would give to all of us.

Jesus is saying that the best things in life are always in danger of being thrown away. What are they? They are love and respect. To love and be loved, to respect and to be respected—these are not pearls to be carried carelessly through the pigpens of this life.

Other pearls are virtue and honesty. Great forces of change are tearing at the very heart of our society. Some of the change is good; but much of it is bad. If the bad changes are not resisted, they can open the gates for the swine to come rushing in.

There are the church and the family. We are prone to cast these aside while at the same time working zealously for our clubs and fraternal organizations. A slighted family can bring about the trampling of the swine. To slight the institution of the church has been a dead-end street for many men.

But the most revealing things that Jesus is saying is that we are always in danger of living a pig's existence. How do we do this? We do this by not wisely choosing what to do with such things as time, health, children, and knowledge. A pig doesn't know the difference between a pearl and scraps. We are always prone to check our real needs in order to satisfy our desires for scraps.

We do this by not having enough courage to change our habits. A pig won't leave the mire. He is not mentally capable. We are at times just like the pig. We talk about knowing better and seeing the need, but we don't change. Then there are others who change for a month or so and then go right back.

We do this by being lazy. This is the laziness of not disciplining ourselves. Why do people live like pigs? It's easier than living like people. These are startling words. We talk of filthy people living like pigs. Here our Lord speaks of something worse—smart, intelligent people who are not in control of their moral life. They can't do anything about it.

I once witnessed a dog chew all afternoon on a shoe. It wasn't worth a cent, but you couldn't prove it to the dog. He lived a dog's existence because he was a dog. "As a man thinketh in his heart, so is he." What do you think of yourself? Have you treasured the real valuables of this life? If not, watch out for the swine!